ith BRINGS AN
EMPTY
Basket

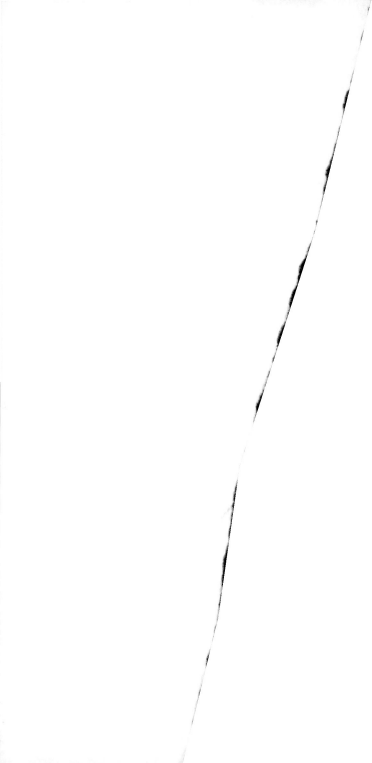

Faith BRINGS AN EMPTY Basket

JOHN S. LEAMAN
DOLLY McELHANEY

WORD AFLAME PRESS

FAITH BRINGS AN EMPTY BASKET
by John S. Leaman and Dolly McElhaney

© 2006 Word Aflame Press
Hazelwood, MO 63042

All Scripture quotations in this book are from the King James Version of the Bible unless otherwise identified.

Names used in various testimonies are fictitious.

Printed in United States of America

Printed by

WORD AFLAME PRESS
8855 Dunn Road, Hazelwood, MO 63042
www.pentecostalpublishing.com

Library of Congress Cataloging-in-Publication Data

Leaman, John S.
    Faith brings an empty basket / by John S. Leaman and Dolly McElhaney.
        p.   cm.
    ISBN-13: 978-1-56722-692-8
    1. Missions—Finance. 2. Christian giving. I. McElhaney, Dolly. II. Title.
BV2081.L43. 2006
248'.6—dc22   2006025518

Contents

To *Edwin E. Judd,*

whose love for the Lord has been demonstrated by his untiring support for those who have said, "Here am I, Lord; send me,"

this book in deep appreciation

is lovingly dedicated.

"Faith promise really works!" John S. Leaman, known to most as "Jack," has declared that message for more than a quarter of a century. We just had our largest month of financial contributions ever. How is this possible? It is because of people like Mr. Faith Promise—Jack Leaman—a man who believes in Faith Promise: breathes it, preaches it, practices it, and now writes about it. Faith Promise works because it blesses the giver and the local church, and it provides a financial reservoir to pay Partners in Missions pledges. It works because Faith Promise helps reach our world. Have you allowed Faith Promise to work for you? If not, try it. It really works! Read on. Be convinced.

Jack Leaman believes in prayer. When I need prayer, I know whom to call: J-A-C-K, and together we can call on J-E-S-U-S.

Jack Leaman lives an impeccable Christian life. Some practice what they preach. Jack preaches what he practices.

Jack Leaman is a giant among men. A Scottish proverb says, "When God measures a man, He puts the tape around his heart and not his head."

Jack Leaman is convinced you cannot outgive God. Like one old farmer said, "I take my shovel and shovel it into God's barn. He takes His shovel and shovels it into my barn. I've learned a simple lesson. God has the biggest shovel!"

Jack Leaman believes in missions. For years he's said, "Some give by going. Others go by giving. Without both there are no missions." Eternity will reveal the impact that Jack and Shirley Leaman have had on the cause of world evangelism. Weekend after weekend they have traversed North America, promoting Faith Promise and sharing hundreds of faith-building testimonies.

Jack Leaman is a world changer. Many people have made the Foreign Missions Division of the UPCI what it is today, and Jack and Shirley Leaman rank close to the top of the list. They left a thriving church and have committed their lives to global missions. Jack and Shirley served on our staff at the World Evangelism Center for twenty-nine years.

Sit back and enjoy the story of how it all began and still continues. You will be challenged to increase your faith and giving. Allow God the opportunity to bless you as you bless our lost world. If you have the faith, God will provide the promise!

—Bruce A. Howell

General Director of Foreign Missions

Introduction

As a young missionary working in India, my coming to the USA for deputational travel was financially important to my future missionary ministry. It was a challenge to raise adequate funds for my next term of service.

Then came the new Partners in Missions program. I was among the first missionaries to be blessed by this program. As pastors became acquainted with the PIM way of supporting missionaries, they received it enthusiastically. Becoming partners with missionaries and supporting them each month with prayer, finance, and letters of encouragement brought a closer relationship between the missionary and the supporting church. When churches received PIM letters from missionaries, they rejoiced.

However, while many pastors wanted to take on more missionaries as partners, their financial resources did not make this possible. When the Faith Promise plan was introduced as the means of raising missionary support, the income for missions in many churches increased from hundreds to thousands of dollars. As this beautiful apostolic plan of giving by faith became an important part of church giving, income increased rapidly and the lives of thousands of men and women in our churches were enriched and blessed spiritually and materially.

In 1976, as Brother John S. Leaman was beginning his service as Director of Promotions for the Foreign Missions Division, I was appointed by the General Board to serve as General Director of Foreign Missions. From that early beginning we worked closely together at World Evangelism Center for the next twenty-five years. My admiration and respect for John Leaman continued to grow as he consistently poured his very life into promoting Faith Promise, setting up schedules for our deputizing missionaries, and doing numerous other large and small tasks in our effort to evangelize the world.

His faithful life of prayer and discipline opened many doors for foreign missions. His zeal and enthusiasm in promoting Faith Promise never dimmed. He traveled all over North America and to some overseas fields, challenging thousands to experience the blessing of Faith Promise giving. He continued collecting stories of how God blessed people who would dare to give by faith.

In this volume we now have a marvelous collection of experiences from across the nation, of people who saw God perform miracles in their own lives. We have long needed this convincing account of how God honors those who bring faith into their giving.

As we read with excitement the numerous accounts of God's miraculous blessing to those who have given by faith, let us remember that as a result of Faith Promise giving, missionaries have had the finance to evangelize the world. Now thousands are baptized in Jesus' name and filled with the Holy Spirit in over 170 nations. Some of our mission fields are now using Faith Promise giving to send forth their own missionaries.

Faith Promise giving makes a difference.

—Harry E. Scism

A person's Faith Promise begins when he or she asks the Lord for direction in the amount of money He would like to channel through them each month for sending and supporting missionaries around the world, and then obeys the leading of the Lord.

Over the years of my preaching on Faith Promise and its benefits, many have approached me to publish the stories of God's blessings on those who had the faith to give. Since my expertise is not in writing, I put off this project, but I prayed much about this need after retiring from full-time work with the Foreign Missions Division.

Dolly McElhaney was hanging out at the Foreign Missions display at the Richmond, Virginia, General Conference when we spotted each other. She had been feeling the prompting of the Spirit to resume writing. I feel that the Lord brought us together for this project. Thus we are making known the testimonies of Faith Promise effectiveness that I have collected over the years.

I pray that the testimonies in this book will challenge and inspire the reader to step out in Faith Promise and help send abroad THE MESSAGE that this world needs.

Faith Promise helps God's people respond to our Lord's great commission.

And if you can't go in person, you can go in purse.

—John S. (Jack) Leaman

A month before the General Conference in Richmond, Virginia, the Lord prepared my heart and mind to resume writing. I had gone from prayer chair to computer desk when a thought washed through me: "It's time to write again." I slipped downstairs and sat on the bed.

"Bill," I said to my half-asleep husband, "I have a confession to make." *That* brought him fully awake!

"I want to write again."

"Good," he answered. "What are you going to write?"

"Don't know," I replied. And I didn't know until a month later when we reached Richmond. As usual, I bee-lined it to the Foreign Missions Division display. Almost immediately, I spotted Shirley Leaman. We shared a hug and chatted a few minutes. As I turned to leave, I almost stepped on Jack Leaman's toes.

"Dolly, you're just the person I want to see!" he exclaimed. "I have all this material for a book, and I don't know what to do with it."

"I do," I said.

Well, I have since repented of my cockiness and smart-alecky answer to Jack, especially after he unloaded over five hundred Faith Promise testimonies for me to sift through, categorize, tie together, and rewrite.

So, Lord, here's my love offering to You.

Let God arise and His enemies be scattered!

—Delores (Dolly) McElhaney

Acknowledgments

First and foremost, I would like to thank the Foreign Missions Division, who thirty years ago gave me the opportunity to work with them as promotions director as well as opening the door for me to travel North America and around the world preaching Faith Promise giving.

So many wonderful people have blessed my life, and I want to express appreciation for some who have been an inspiration in writing this book.

I was blessed to be born into a Pentecostal home with wonderful parents who loved and supported missionaries long before Faith Promise was introduced to the fellowship.

My brother Paul's church was a top-ten-giving missions' supporter, and I always wanted to be just like him. After graduating from Bible school, I was blessed to be an assistant to R. G. Cook who, as a Foreign Missions Board member, brought many missionaries by the church, thus exposing me to a world beyond North America. This only whetted my appetite to do more for the missionary.

My wife has been a great blessing to me for over forty-nine years, has traveled with me to many churches at home and abroad, and has helped me write this book.

Dolly McElhaney with her expert ability has been an answer to prayer in the writing of this book. We have been friends for many years since youth camp in Ohio.

We've spent many hours through email and telephone in putting these stories together.

Many pastors opened their church doors to having Faith Promise presented to their congregations, and numerous individuals heard the Word and responded by allowing God to miraculously supply. They then kindly sent me their testimonies.

Harry Scism, Edwin Judd, and Bruce Howell inspired me to record the steps of faith that many have taken, with their amazing results.

—Jack Leaman

To Brian Abernathy, Bruce Howell, and Margie McNall, who helped me get back into the swing of (writing) things;

To my wonderful friends of the Rarity Bay Ladies' Bible Study group who unceasingly prayed for me, and endured my using them as a sounding board;

To my daughter Lisa, a remarkable writer in her own right, who prods, and chides, and pokes, and exercises pithy editorial comment;

And to Bill, always Bill, who fixes his own sandwiches and closes his eyes to dust on the furniture and lets me clatter away at the computer while he mucks the horse's stall, thereby earning a type of sainthood just for being my husband for forty-seven years;

Thank you.

—Dolly McElhaney

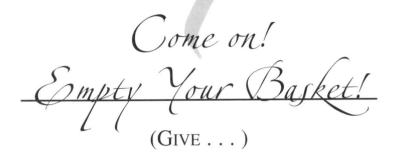

Come on!
Empty Your Basket!
(GIVE . . .)

God is the original Grandmaster of giving. He made man out of the dust of the ground and *gave* man life by breathing into his nostrils.

Then God planted the most incredible garden eastward in Eden—and *gave* it to the man!

God then anesthetized the man, and from a rib, He shaped a woman—and *gave* her to the man to be his partner through life.

Through the ages, God kept on *giving:* deliverance of the Israelites from Egypt, laws that made twelve tribes a nation and established a religion, an inheritance in a promised land, and finally, centuries later, as the apostle John recorded, God *gave* His only begotten Son . . . who *gave* Himself for us. . . .

A man with no job heard this message of a giving God when he wandered into a church where members of the congregation were promising to commit a certain amount of money each week or month to send and support missionaries overseas.

"Give, and it shall be given unto you," the pastor assured the congregation. "God will be no man's debtor for long."

We'll see about that, the man thought. *I have no job, no income. My wife has left me. My daughters have left me. And I'm in debt. So I'll just prove God. I'll find out if what that pastor is saying is true.*

So the man signed a Faith Promise card to give a certain percent of his nonexistent income to God through missions.

Within hours, he had a job! And when he got his first paycheck, he faithfully gave the percent he had promised.

A diligent, hardworking person, before long he got a raise. He decided to give a bit more to missions.

Then he got a better job, one that paid him more money. Month after month, he gave as he had promised. Before too long, he bought a nice suit and could dress better.

Then wonderful things began to happen.

His wife came back.

So did his daughters.

Before many months passed, he had paid every debt.

His salary was raised yet again.

He later testified, "I am a prosperous businessman. I own my own home, I have money in the bank, and I am not in debt."

The man had brought an empty basket. By faith he offered it to God. And God had filled it: good measure, pressed down, shaken together, and running over.

The full verse of Luke 6:38 reads, "Give, and it shall be given unto you; good measure, pressed down, and shaken together, and running over, shall men give into your bosom. For with the same measure that ye mete withal it shall be measured to you again." That verse has waved like a banner over Jack Leaman's ministry. That verse has also been an unshakable foundation under him to both practice and preach.

Luke 6:38 has waved like a banner over Jack Leaman's ministry.

One day while Jack was pastoring in Lancaster, Ohio, a young man came to him.

"Brother Leaman," Mike stated, "I have a problem. I made a Faith Promise commitment, but I've lost my job. What shall I do? How can I keep my commitment when I have no job?"

"Mike, I believe God has a better job for you."

A few days later, Mike pulled Jack aside. "Brother Leaman, you were right! God has given me a better job. Now I can keep my promise to the Lord."

In a short time, Mike was back. Jack fully expected him to say he had received some sort of financial blessing, but that was not the case.

"Brother Leaman," he moaned, "I lost that good job. My boss wanted me to tell a lie, and I refused. Now what should I do?"

"I believe God has an even better job for you," Jack replied. "You lost your job because you upheld a principle of God. He won't let you down."

And He didn't. Within a few more days Mike stopped Jack at church. He was very excited. "Brother Leaman, I have another job, and it's the best job I've ever had!"

During Jack's pastorate in Lancaster, he learned through his brother, Paul, of a recently introduced, systematic method for raising funds for missionaries.

"It's called Faith Promise, Jack," Paul explained. "Individuals in the congregation agree to give foreign missions x number of dollars a month. The church can then help support a missionary, becoming a partner in missions with him. Such consistent giving allows the missionary to operate from a stable base. Remember hearing the stories some of our missionaries tell? They manage to do a tremendous work for God with only fitful, sporadic offerings. Think how many more souls could be reached if each missionary had an income he could rely on!"

"Are you using the Faith Promise idea?" Jack asked his brother, immediately realizing the tremendous blessing Faith Promise could be to missionary families.

"Yes," Paul replied. "I am. Brother Tenney is behind it one hundred percent. Brother Lorian Hedger is doing a fantastic job with the idea out in the Western District. We had a district conference in Lancaster one year. Brother Judd represented the Foreign Missions Division and introduced the Partners in Missions and Faith Promise programs there. Brother Tommy Craft spoke at night, and missionaries Harry Scism and Billy Cole were present.

Both missionaries received many partners during that conference. Then Brother Judd explained both concepts to my church, and it has increased our missions giving tremendously."

"What about other churches here in Ohio? Are any of them involved?" Jack was curious.

"Brother Kinzie in Toledo jumped on it. So did Brother Paul Cook in Columbus," Paul Leaman said.

Jack needed no further encouragement to try Faith Promise in the Lancaster church. He implemented the fledgling program at the First Apostolic Church by holding a Missionary Faith Promise weekend with missionary Paul Reynolds from Jamaica presenting the program to the church. The tremendous response started a Faith Promise ministry that allowed the church to become a partner in missions with several missionaries. However, some of the saints questioned using the money for missions when the local church had so many needs of its own.

"Brother Leaman, how can you do this to the church?"

One day shortly after the Faith Promise weekend, a Sunday school teacher who taught a junior class drew Jack aside. From the look on the man's face, Jack could see he was upset.

"Brother Leaman, how can you do this to the church?" the man asked.

"What do you mean? What have I done?" Jack asked in return.

"You presented this Faith Promise thing for foreign missions, but we have so many needs right here in our church. Think what we could do with the money here!"

"Let's see what will happen," Jack counseled. "Why don't you get your Sunday school class involved? Have your class write to missionaries. Tack a missionary map on the wall in your classroom and let the kids choose a missionary to pray for. Keep track of how many souls are being baptized in Jesus' name and being filled with the Holy Ghost as a result of your involvement with the missionary."

Still doubtful, the man shook his head as he moved away. But he followed Jack's suggestions and interested his class in missions.

Before many weeks passed, the teacher again pulled Jack aside. "Brother Leaman! Do you know what is happening in our Sunday school class? We decided to raise funds for the missionaries, and the kids have been receiving the Holy Ghost, right in class on Sunday mornings!"

Many children walked directly from that class to be baptized during the morning worship service. And their teacher became not only a strong giver to missions but also a prosperous businessman.

While in Lancaster, Jack had been asked to assume the role of youth president for the Ohio District. Jack zigzagged across Ohio to promote various missions' projects as the state broke their Sheaves for Christ effort for a number of years. As youth president, he initiated a program that used Bible school students to intern in churches during the summer months, giving the students experience and the home mission churches some help in reaching their communities, all the while promoting Sheaves for Christ.

As the result of the congregation's fasting and prayer, revivals, and tent meetings on the fairgrounds, by the end of 1975 attendance had grown to averaging 464. The faithfulness of the membership in reaching out to others contributed greatly to this growth. One five-week revival with evangelist Lee Stoneking saw sixty-five receive the Holy Ghost, including Jack's son and daughter. The Lancaster church was one of the largest in Ohio. It was eleventh in the nation in foreign missions giving. Of the top eleven churches in the nation in foreign missions giving, five of those churches were in Ohio.

Of the top eleven churches in the nation in foreign missions giving, five of those churches were in Ohio.

"Foreign Missions had several board members who knew this, and when the door opened for a replacement for director of promotions in the division, I was asked if I would consider that position," Jack relates. "But the Lancaster church was in revival, so I said no."

Then a second call came: "Brother Leaman, we'd like you to come and be our promotional director."

"No," Jack said again. "The church here is absolutely thriving. I can't leave it."

A third phone call: "Brother Leaman, what will it take for you to come and join the team with Foreign Missions?"

"I would have to know that such a move is in the will of God," Jack replied. "Besides, I don't want to uproot my family. My son is fifteen and my daughter is twelve. Those are precarious ages for young people."

More calls came. Jack sought advice from his wife, Shirley; his brother, Paul; and most of all, from the Lord. He talked to his children. Finally he made the trip to St. Louis to find out what would be expected of him there. When he returned to Lancaster, he felt that he should accept the offer and assume the responsibilities of promotions director for the Foreign Missions Division of the United Pentecostal Church.

Lancaster, Ohio: an ending.
St. Louis, Missouri: a beginning.

The cities are 450 miles apart by the map, but Jack's jobs in those cities are a thousand miles apart in responsibilities. As Jack sat in the airport in Columbus, Ohio, in February 1976, waiting for the plane to St. Louis, he thought back over his ministry while wondering what lay in store. He had always been involved in pastoring. What would his change in ministry entail?

He would have to learn many new skills.

He would be scheduling missionaries across North America in their deputation travels.

He would be promoting Faith Promise and Partners in Missions around the world.

He would achingly miss the beloved saints in Lancaster.

His whole way of life would be upended.

But he would never feel that he had missed the will of God in taking this position.

With the help of the brethren in St. Louis, Jack began to feel comfortable in his new duties. But discomfort niggled him when it came to scheduling Faith Promise services. Jack came to think of this as the FOG, or Fear Of Giving, syndrome. Many pastors, seeing the needs of their own congregations, felt like the Sunday school teacher in the Lancaster church: "Brother Leaman, how can you do this to the church?"

Jack came to think of this as the FOG, or Fear Of Giving, syndrome.

At those times, he clung to the testimonies of those pastors who had experienced the immeasurable blessings of giving beyond themselves and their own church's needs. He recalled what had happened to Paul Cook in 1974. Paul staunchly supported Faith Promise, and he reported:

> For many years the Groveport, Ohio, church had annual Faith Promise services, which resulted in the church's giving to missions. For a number of years, we were sixth or seventh nationally in our giving. At that time our Sunday school attendance was approximately 250.
>
> In 1974, we were making plans to build

when a man called me to meet with him. This man was a millionaire businessman who, after coming to the Lord, wanted to build a church center. On fifty-four acres of land, he built a church sanctuary, a youth center, and a four-bedroom home. He also purchased five new, sixty-six-passenger buses. After trying to build a congregation, he visited our church and, seeing our growth, asked me if I would be interested in taking over what he had created. He handed me a list of assets valued at approximately a million dollars. Our group voted to receive this gift, and we moved into this location. Within a year, our attendance increased into the three hundreds.

We sincerely thanked the Lord for this miracle and also thanked Him for blessing our giving to missions.

The Beginnings of the Faith Promise Concept

Shored by such a testimony and thinking about his own experience in Lancaster with the Faith Promise concept, Jack sought out Edwin Judd.

"Brother Judd, you are such a believer in the Faith Promise idea," Jack said. "You have really promoted the concept. What do you know of its history?"

"In the early '60s, Orion Gleason, my brother-in-law, handed me a little booklet that had been given to him by a non-UPC pastor. It was titled *Triumphant Missionary Ministry in the Local Church*, and was published by Back to the Bible Broadcast. The booklet analyzed the factors

24

common to major missions-supporting churches of all persuasions," Brother Judd explained. "A study of this subject had indicated that all such churches had an annual missions' convention and used the faith promise concept. It further gave a brief explanation of the concept.

"John E. Klemin was pastoring the First United Pentecostal Church in Portland and I was pastoring the UPC in Vancouver, Washington. We discussed the faith promise idea and decided to practice this between our churches. Two other nearby churches joined us in participating in a missions' convention and used the faith promise concept. The Conquerors Bible College staff and student body were involved in this joint venture inasmuch as they attended the various churches involved. However, the student body was encouraged to make their commitment through the college missions' fund as agreed upon by the pastors involved. There was tremendous unity in this joint effort and total cooperation.

"The first year we had Paul H. Box, then Foreign Missions secretary, as our convention speaker. Oscar Vouga, Foreign Missions director, was our speaker in one of those early conventions. Both of these men witnessed the presentation of Faith Promise and the results of these conventions. I had developed a response brochure and other materials to promote the concept among our people locally.

"Then, in the summer of 1967, Brother Vouga approached me.

"'Brother Judd,' he asked, 'would you consider leaving the presidency of Conquerors Bible College to come to headquarters for the purpose of introducing the Faith Promise concept to the UPCI fellowship?'

"After prayerful consideration, at the 1967 General Conference I agreed to do so at the end of the school year in 1968, and made the move to Saint Louis in June of that year."

"What were some of the things you did after you moved to Saint Louis?" Jack asked.

"During my first fifteen months at headquarters, I concentrated on developing materials and promoting Faith Promise. Among the first pastors to open their doors to the idea were Paul Cook, Fred Kinzie, Al McNally, your brother, Paul, and a host of others. By early 1969, we determined that we needed some program to lead our churches in greater commitment to consistent missions' support, and Partners in Missions was born. It was introduced at the General Conference in 1969 in the Sunday night service. Brother T. F. Tenney was elected Foreign Missions director the next day. Because I was with Foreign Missions at Brother Vouga's invitation, I offered my resignation to Brother Tenney. He promptly refused it, and together we launched the introduction of Faith Promise and Partner in Missions."

"You said that a forerunner of the idea was born in Oregon. Was any program promoting missions still going on in the West and Northwest?" Jack wanted to know.

Brother Judd thought a moment before replying. "Just how and when the brethren in the Western District were introduced to the Faith Promise concept and began to promote it in their district, I do not know. I do know that Lorian Hedger did a tremendous job of promoting foreign missions in the Western District while he held that position."

"Do you know where the idea originated in the first place?" Jack asked.

Judd nodded. "A. B. Simpson, founder of the Christian Missionary and Alliance Church, started it. When someone tried to give him credit for it, he said he got it from the apostle Paul, basically from Second Corinthians, chapters eight and nine, and Philippians chapter four. I have in my library a book of missionary messages by A. B. Simpson, one of which is titled 'The Grace of Giving' and is a message from these three chapters. It is quite an exposition on Faith Promise."

"So the idea did not originate in our fellowship," Jack said.

"No, it didn't. But by whatever means it has come to be implemented, it has been a tremendous instrument to bring blessing to many and make many a blessing to the fulfillment of the great commission.

"Let me give you some figures on that," Brother Judd continued. "In 1963 when I was appointed to the Foreign Missions Board, the total UPCI foreign missions budget was approximately $350,000. When I went to St. Louis five years later, this budget was $475,000."

Jack wondered what the income for foreign missions had been for 1975. Upon checking the records, he discovered that with the increased promotion using Faith Promise and Partners in Missions, the offerings for foreign missions between 1968 and 1975 had grown to

$3,116,253, an increase of nearly 700 percent! Moreover, 165 missionaries and 42 short-term missionaries were reaching 66 nations with the gospel.

T. F. Tenney, Edwin Judd, and Harry Scism were a tremendous blessing in the Leaman family's adjustment to a new place, a new church, a new home, and new job responsibilities. But Jack lacked opportunities to explain Faith Promise and Partners in Missions. Pastors were

Giving to foreign missions increased by 700% between 1968 and 1975.

reluctant to sponsor a program that they felt would draw income from the churches they pastored. Jack had used Faith Promise in Lancaster and could relate testimonies from the church he once pastored, so he felt quite confident that the Lord would bless individuals, pastors, and churches if they would step out in faith concerning their giving. He chafed at the restrictions to growth and blessing he believed pastors were unwittingly putting on their congregations. He prayed against the fear of giving that gripped the church leaders.

In 1976, few churches held Faith Promise services. Many churches supported missionaries, but they did not understand the concept of Faith Promise. Jack went with another minister to Toronto, Ontario, Canada, to see what a church of another denomination did to launch out with the concept. This church held a weeklong conference bringing in many nationals, missionaries, and others to expose their church to reaching beyond the North American continent. *This church gave globally, and God blessed them locally.* They modeled sacrificial giving to reach others. Jack was impressed that they did not show material wealth but a burden for the lost. After that trip, he even used the Canadian church as an example of giving to others. Soon he was able to use testimonies from UPCI churches!

Breakthrough!

At last a breakthrough came for Jack. Pastor Eugene McClintock of Mt. Vernon, Illinois, scheduled a Faith Promise service on March 7, 1976. It was a Faith Promise first for both men since Jack had come to the office.

"The response in Faith Promise commitments was $720.25," Leaman recalls. "Brother McClintock seemed quite pleased. I was, too."

Then, on April 4, Jack preached in Groves, Texas. Later, Jack learned that a couple there had just come into the church. They had been baptized but had not received the Holy Ghost.

"Brother Leaman, the husband checked to see how much he and his wife had been spending on cigarettes and drink," the pastor reported. "They made their commitment for the same amount."

Jack felt a tingle of anticipation. "Has God blessed them some way?" he asked.

"I'll say!" the pastor reported. "The husband just received the Holy Ghost!"

By the middle of May 1976, Jack had held four more

Faith Promise services: in Michigan; Texas; Ontario, Canada; and North Carolina. These services, set so far apart geographically, allowed pastors and churches in different parts of the country to learn about Faith Promise. He felt encouraged, too, because he had thirteen more services scheduled during the year.

Legionnaires' Disease, earthquakes, the Olympics, a new religion founded by Sun Myung Moon, and the election of Democratic candidate Jimmy Carter filled the news while Jack visited ten more districts and exposed them to the concepts and principles of Faith Promise and Partners in Missions. Then, just before Thanksgiving and within one week's time, he received two letters that sent his heart swelling with joy.

One pastor wrote that even though the church was still averaging around 150, their foreign missions giving had been extraordinary. In the first month after their missions' service, their monthly offering had increased by $450! The average of the church's monthly giving had

In one family, four members had received the Holy Ghost, and the husband had found a job.

reached just over $700. In one family, four members had received the Holy Ghost, and the husband had found a job. A lady with an unsaved husband gave to missions. Her car developed a knocking rod. Three mechanics all diagnosed the same problem. When she pulled into the repair station, the banging stopped! She shifted into reverse and drove away. That had been several months ago, but the problem had not returned.

The second letter had a different slant to it. A lady wrote that she had decided to raise her commitment by $2, knowing full well that only through faith could she pay it.

> God not only supplied the money but He also provided for our family and touched us in a very beautiful way. Our youngest son, then about ten months old, had surgery to remove what was thought to be a cyst on his eyelid. We later found out it was not a cyst but a blood tumor, and cutting into it started it to grow. Doctors began to talk of surgery to remove the tumor and plastic surgery to replace the eyelid, or use of an experimental drug that had never been used on a child so small. The drug was known to eat away bone when used in excess. We were sick with despair.

So the family took the problem to the Lord. The doctors gave them four months to see what would happen before setting a date for surgery. Nothing changed in the four months, but six months after that, hardly anything was visible of the tumor.

God had supplied the money for that year, but when time for a new Faith Promise came, the woman took stock of her finances: her tithes had doubled, she'd met her previous commitment, paid her bills, and even put money in savings for the first time in six years of marriage.

The night we were signing our card I felt terrible. I was unsettled but couldn't decide why. When I prayed before signing the Faith Promise card, I felt God tell me what He wanted me to give. My first impression was, "Impossible! I don't have that much! Where would it come from?" Then I felt a beautiful calm come over me and I realized that was the key. I would give it by *faith* and God would provide. I did and He did.

A week later, the woman began to receive a weekly income that was $10 over the amount of her weekly Faith Promise. That same week, she received a letter from an organization she'd never heard of, telling her of a new law passed that entitled her up to $150 a month of tax-free money from the federal government. All she had to do was file some papers. "I don't worry about money problems now because I've a professional bookkeeper!" she concluded.

The Testimonies Continue

Finally, another breakthrough came. On January 20, 1977, Jimmy Carter was inaugurated as the thirty-ninth President of the United States. Three days later, Jack was in Gary, Indiana, and the weekend was outstanding. A saleslady in the congregation ventured her first Faith Promise commitment. Afterward, she wrote Jack, saying, "The first month following my commitment, my override was $80! I had never before received an override from my sales. The next month it was $800.

The next month it was over $1,000, and it hasn't been under $1,000 a month since!"

That lady was later promoted to manager.

An encouraging letter Jack received on January 31 from a pastor in the Midwest further bolstered his confidence. The letter traced the path of God's supplying their Faith Promise for 1975 and 1976.

In November, the pastor and his wife agreed to give $1,000 to missions the following year. The pastor's wife had had surgery for bone cancer in September, and the bill came in shortly after the Faith Promise service. The insurance company refused to pay the $1,100 for the medical bills because the woman had had an even earlier bout with cancer.

Then, in December, the pastor was able to sell one of their cars at a $500 profit. They paid all of this on Faith Promise, trying to believe God for the $1,100 medical bills.

On January 1, they decided to pay the balance of their Faith Promise in monthly payments from their income. Two weeks later, a fine Baptist lady called to ask if they had a special need, stating that God had told her to give them $500. When the lady came to church on February 1, she brought a $500 check made out to the pastor.

The pastor and his wife finished paying their Faith Promise.

On February 15, the same lady called again, saying she wanted to give them $200 more.

"By this time, I could believe God for anything!" the pastor said. At that point they were paying monthly payments on the medical bills.

On March 1, the Baptist lady returned to church, but instead of $200, she gave them another $500! They had already paid their Faith Promise, so they put this on the medical bills. Then, to their happy surprise, the insurance company reconsidered and paid them for half of the medical bills, which paid the bill in full.

The most exciting thing is that fifty people have been baptized and fifty have received the Holy Ghost!

A month or two later, Jack held another service in Texas, with amazing results. The pastor sent Jack a letter.

> Brother Leaman, since you were here five months ago, a remarkable thing has happened. I was afraid that giving to missions would reduce our offerings in other areas, but that is not the case. Our Home Missions, Ladies' Ministry, Harvestime, and Sheaves for Christ offerings have all been up. But the most exciting thing is that fifty people have been baptized and fifty have received the Holy Ghost!

In April of 1977, Leaman's second year as director of promotions, John Benson, at that time the Texas District Foreign Missions Director, invited Jack and Harry Scism to travel throughout Texas. For two weeks the three men climbed into Benson's 1975 burgundy Oldsmobile and drove from section to section, visiting a number of churches. Interest in Faith Promise and Partners in Missions rolled through dusty Texas like tumbleweeds on the wind, and it thrilled the three men to see the Lord work in outstanding ways.

As funds were being raised during a missions' rally in a Texas church, the pastor himself made a commitment.

After the service a second pastor walked up to the host pastor who had just made a commitment for the offering in that service.

"Brother, do you need a bus?" came the unexpected question.

"Need a bus?" the local pastor replied. "Do we ever! The bus we have is so bad, a cat with any self-respect wouldn't make his home in it!"

"Well, we have a bus we'd like to give you," the other pastor said.

"Brother Leaman," the excited pastor stammered, "I just made a commitment in this service, and look what has happened!"

Little did the three men know that of all the testimonies they would later gather from their trek through Texas, few would top Benson's own.

At that time Benson was starting a church in Euless, Texas. The small home missions church had received an insurance bill for $657 and did not have the money to pay it. However, Benson's church was involved in Faith Promise.

When Benson returned home at the end of the two weeks of services, he found a package in the mail. He opened the package to reveal a grocery bag folded inside.

With trembling fingers, Benson unfolded the bag. He reached in and pulled out a wad of money. When he counted the money, he discovered $660 with a statement saying, "To a servant of the Lord." Benson couldn't find a name anywhere in the package.

Jack knew that if he could present giving in a way that people would understand it, he could "sell" Faith Promise with outstanding results.

During that second year, Leaman held thirty-seven Faith Promise services in eight more districts. He introduced Faith Promise to more and more pastors and showed them how it could bless them and their churches in so many ways. He fasted often and prayed continuously that the Lord would give him a greater understanding of Faith Promise. He had once been a salesman for Sears, Roebuck and Company and knew that if he could present giving in a way that the churches would understand it, he could "sell" Faith Promise with outstanding results. He had been number one in sales in four of the five years that he had worked at Sears while in Wisconsin. He decided to put those skills to work.

To be successful in selling you must sell people on the product, he mused. *You must convince the client beyond a shadow of a doubt. If I can present Faith Promise with examples of how it works, the Lord will honor His Word. How can I help people understand that if they step out in faith in their giving, the Lord will honor their faith and provide the funds they have trusted Him for?*

Leaman kept a record of Faith Promise services from the start. Then, as testimonies verifying Luke 6:38 rolled in and piled up, he realized that the Lord was filling the baskets that had been emptied for His sake.

A man in Ohio testified that when Faith Promise time came around, he had no job and no prospects of one. Before the service, he had decided not to renew his commitment and just give as he got money to do so. While he sat in church and prayed about the matter, God let him know to go ahead with his Faith Promise as if he had a job, and to count on Him to provide the funds so the man could keep his promise.

The next morning, his wife handed him a phone number from the newspaper.

"Why don't you try this number?" she asked.

He called and was given a well-paying job that enabled him to work with his teenage son. Then he met two men who needed some extra work done. Those two jobs netted him $865, more than his Faith Promise commitment. All of this came within the first month after he renewed his commitment!

The testimony thrilled Jack. "I felt that the Lord had given me a better understanding of Faith Promise, and I began to promote it more effectively," he says. "The Lord was honoring the preaching of His Word and I felt to preach it all the more fervently. Even more doors opened as pastors began to realize that giving is a part of living, and that when they open their church doors to the preaching of giving, God blesses their own ministry and their saints in every way."

While driving one day, Jack heard a curious thought expressed on the radio.

"Giving is part of living," the speaker said. "If you don't believe that, try taking a deep breath and holding it. Now take another deep breath without first giving out your previous one! It can't be done because you must give so you can live."

Jack thought of the lad in the Bible who had emptied his own little basket of five loaves and two small fish, and how the Lord had blessed and multiplied that emptying.

The disciples gathered up twelve basketsful after the five thousand had been fed, Jack mused. *And that little, nameless boy was written about by all the Gospel writers. How he must have impressed the disciples!*

Lord, please help me to show others that only by emptying ourselves of ourselves, can we be truly filled.

Why Are You So Surprised?

(. . . AND IT SHALL BE GIVEN UNTO YOU . . .)

Emptying one's self of self is not easy, Jack continued to muse, *but when it happens, miracles occur.*

His thoughts drifted to the tales of two widows in the Bible. One widow emptied her purse of the two pitiable mites in it, an offering of one-quarter of a cent, yet it was her living. The other widow, not having even the smallest coin, scraped the bottom of the barrel and watched the last drop of oil drip from a cruse in order to feed a traveling missionary-prophet named Elijah.

As long as there is a Bible, he thought, *those two women will be remembered. Unnamed, they nevertheless have their stories written in God's imperishable Word. They will never be forgotten.*

Jack's files contained a tale of two other, very different widows who attended the same Faith Promise service. One lady had very little income; the other was a millionaire. The poor lady put her faith in the Lord to help her eke out $10 a month to give to missions. The millionaire woman promised to give $1 a month.

The poor woman's son, impressed by his mother's faith and spirit of giving, decided to pay her Faith Promise for her. Two years later, the woman became very ill. Though feeble from illness, she managed to come to a Wednesday night service and asked to be prayed for. God not only healed her of that ailment, but He also touched and healed the deafness in one of her ears.

The wealthy widow? In the same two years she had grown increasingly senile and had been placed in a nursing home. She knew nothing of what went on—not even that her family was having a grand time spending her money!

A third widow, not knowing how she could possibly pay the $40 a month she committed, put her trust in the Lord. She had some schoolbooks she wanted to sell, so she took them to the mall. The $640 she netted from the sale far exceeded her expectations. She not only was able to pay the entire year's Faith Promise, but her tithes as well. She even contributed the balance to the church's building fund!

The following story parallels—up to a point—the tale of the widow who dropped the last two mites that she had into the Temple treasury. In the modern setting, the two mites are two dollars, but here's the story:

A missionary called ahead to the district Foreign Missions director to get his schedule of churches he would be visiting in that district.

"We're having our district conference that week," the director told the missionary, "but come and enjoy the conference. Maybe we can get some Partners in Missions for you at the conference."

The missionary arrived at the conference with a total of $2 in his pocket. When the offering was being taken, the Lord spoke to the missionary to put the $2 in the offering.

Lord, it's all I have. And with no services scheduled for the rest of this week, even the two dollars I have is mighty little to live on, he argued. Nevertheless, when the offering basket passed in front of him, he dropped the rolled-up bills in it. Then, his conscience clear, he pushed all other thoughts aside to join in the service.

Later in the same service the district superintendent startled the missionary by saying that they had a missionary at the conference.

"I want to take up an offering for the missionary," the district superintendent declared.

After service the district Foreign Missions director walked up to the missionary.

"I know you missed having services this week," he said with a smile. "Maybe this offering will help." He handed the offering to the missionary.

Stunned, the missionary looked in awe at the amount of money gripped in his hand.

The offering was exactly $1,002.

"Once upon a time" may start many children's fairy tales, but the phrase could also introduce stirring Bible stories and riveting, present-day testimonies of God at work. During the year, another story of almost fairy-tale proportions had come to Jack's office.

A Texas lady who lived in a college town befriended some exchange students from Saudi Arabia and took them into her home to live. From time to time, she also let them drive her car. They seemed grateful to be allowed to use the old thing, battered and rattling as it was. Eventually the young men returned to their home country. She continued to drive her old car for another year or so until it became evident that it was on its last wheels.

Her church had scheduled a Faith Promise service. While she listened to the sermon, she debated within herself whether she should renew her Faith Promise or use the money to make monthly payments on a new car, which by then she desperately needed.

She prayed—and renewed her commitment.

Not long after the service, one of the men from Saudi Arabia who had stayed in her home returned to the city and came to the Ford garage where she worked as a secretary.

He greeted her warmly and then asked, "Do you still drive that beat-up old car?"

Smiling, she said she did. They chatted for a few minutes more and then she returned to her office.

The man sought out a salesperson and ran his hand over the glossy surface of a yellow LTD Ford on the showroom floor.

"I want to give her this car," he told the salesperson and then pointed to her office. "Please service this car for her and have it ready for her to drive home after work."

His thankful generosity didn't stop with giving the

woman a new car. He walked to her office and laid a lovely new watch on her desk. Then he handed her $200!

"For gas," he said, and left.

Jack smiled to himself at the testimony. He had been in Oklahoma in a service months after that event and told the congregation what God had done for that lady. After he finished his sermon, an elderly man stood and asked if he could say something.

The "something" was this: "It was my sister who received the new car," the man reported, as oooh's and aaah's of surprise rippled through the congregation.

Why are people so surprised when God keeps His promise? Jack wondered. He recalled several testimonies in which people had expressed their astonishment at the way God helped them meet their Faith Promise. He remembered a service where a very excited lady rushed to talk to him afterwards.

"Brother Leaman," she said, "I have no income. My husband was killed in an automobile accident, and he had not paid enough into Social Security for me to receive any benefits. I live with my parents, and that is how I survive.

She had been given ten months of her Faith Promise commitment before she even left the church!

"Tonight, though, I felt that the Lord impressed me to make a $10 per month Faith Promise. Remember how we all gathered around the altar to pray after you preached?

Well, when I walked back to my seat and opened my purse, I found a hundred-dollar bill! That's ten months of my commitment before I even walk out the door of the church tonight!"

Later Jack learned that a lady in the choir felt impressed to slip that bill into the widow's purse.

A brother in the Lord nearly stuttered in his excitement as he told Jack what had happened to him.

"Brother Leaman, God has blessed us so much I am overwhelmed!" the man said. "I had become rather discouraged with my pay and was looking for another job when I made my Faith Promise commitment. The very next day my boss called me into his office and said, 'We can't afford to lose you.'

"They raised my pay by two dollars an hour but asked me to keep quiet about it. A few days later, everyone got a raise, so I got another dollar an hour raise. Within the month of my commitment, I received raises totaling three dollars and sixty cents an hour! On top of it all, my wife also got a raise. I can hardly believe it!"

After a Sunday night Faith Promise service a young man walked up to Jack to report a rather unusual way in which God had met his need.

"Brother Leaman," he said, "I've just got to tell you what happened to me after last year's service! When I walked into the vestibule of the church the night of the Faith Promise service, the Lord impressed on me how much I was to commit.

"Brother Leaman, it was double what I'd been planning

to give! I was going to sign my Faith Promise card for twenty five dollars, so I questioned the Lord about the fifty dollars a month. I'm going to electrical school, and with my studies, I can only work fifteen hours a week. I wanted to obey the Lord, though, so I wrote fifty dollars a month. That was a big step of faith for me!

"Two days later my boss came up to me.

"'Let's go get a cup of coffee and a piece of pie,' my boss said.

"Brother Leaman, would you believe it? While we were eating, my boss told me that over the weekend he had felt impressed to start paying me for forty hours' pay for fifteen hours of work. Can you beat that? My pay increase was four times a week what my monthly Faith Promise had been!

"I was shocked and delighted, but of course I knew why it had happened."

Jack himself was amazed when he learned that a seventy-two-year-old widow had promised the Lord that she would give $250 a month to foreign missions. *Many people spread $250 over an entire year's giving,* he thought. *But $3000 a year? That's a sizeable sum for an elderly widow lady to commit to the Lord.*

Curious about the lady and her situation, Jack wondered how well she was doing in keeping her Faith Promise. So he asked her pastor.

"Oh," her pastor replied to Jack's query, "that little lady is very faithful in keeping her commitment."

"How does she manage to pay so much?" Jack asked. "Is she a wealthy lady?"

"No, not at all," her pastor replied. He began to chuckle. "You'll never guess what she does to keep that commitment." He paused. "She works."

"What kind of work can a seventy-two-year-old widow do?" Jack asked.

"She takes care of old folks," the pastor said, and Jack could hear the tickled-pink tone in the pastor's voice. "Right now she's taking care of a lady 109 years old."

Tales of Six Saints

The unusual seems to be "just the usual" with the Lord. The following testimonies fall into the "strange but true" category. First, who would ever dream that broken false teeth would pay for a Faith Promise? Second, can you imagine being asked to loan someone the money so he could pay his Faith Promise? Third, a pastor found the well of his faith deepened considerably. Fourth, an accountant found his Faith Promise in a pocket—his! Fifth, a telephone call surprised a college student. And finally, a pastor bagged a bounty when a business failed. As improbable as it seems, all six tales happened.

Story 1: A woman fell while shopping. To her dismay, her dentures popped out of her mouth, smashed against the hard floor, and broke. Replacing them would be expensive, but she had to have teeth!

Disregarding the cost of replacing her dentures when Faith Promise time rolled around, she trusted the Lord for a commitment of $50 a month.

Shortly afterwards, the store manager phoned her.

"Ma'am, would you settle for five thousand dollars?"

came the unexpected and startling question.

"But I have no intention of suing the store," she assured the store manager. "You don't have to worry about that."

"Thank you, ma'am, but we want to settle this," the official insisted. "Would you accept five thousand dollars?"

Would she! Even after paying for the new dentures, she had plenty of money left to keep her Faith Promise for the whole year!

Story 2: A pastor was very happy when a visitor expressed a desire to give $100 to the church.

Then the visitor shocked the pastor.

"May I borrow one hundred dollars?" he asked.

"Let me get this straight," the pastor replied. "You want to borrow one hundred dollars so you can give the church one hundred dollars?"

"That's right," the visitor said.

I may never see this money again, the pastor thought, *but this man's request is so weird I'm going to go along with it.*

So the pastor obliged and gave him the requested one hundred dollars.

A week later the pastor received a letter from the man. When he opened the envelope and unfolded the note inside, a check for $1,100 fell out.

"Five hundred dollars is for the church," the note read, "and five hundred dollars is for you. The other one hundred dollars is to repay the money you loaned me last week."

Marveling, the pastor deposited the money in the bank.

The check did not bounce.

Story 3: A minister who was deeply involved in overseeing the building of a new church structure was contacted about having a missionary service.

"I'd like to have the service," the pastor told the district Foreign Missions director, "but we can't take the missionary on as a full partner. We'll have to have a well drilled very soon, and we've been quoted a price of two thousand dollars. We'll have to scrape to find that much money."

Nevertheless, during the service the pastor felt led to take the missionary on with PIM support even though they didn't have the money. He obeyed what he felt impressed to commit and took the missionary on for $15 a month. It was not as much as the pastor wanted to give, but it was a start.

Shortly after the service with the missionary, the time came to drill the well.

And very shortly after that the pastor's phone rang.

"Reverend?" a deep voice asked. "I understand your church needs to have a well drilled."

"Yes, we have reached that point," the pastor admitted.

"We'd like to have your business," the caller continued.

"We'll consider it," the pastor declared, hoping the man's bid would be less than the two-thousand-dollar bid they had already received.

"We'll do it for fifty dollars," the man said.

"Fifty dollars!" the pastor exclaimed. "But . . . who? . . . what? . . . how?"

"We are a drilling school," the man explained. "If you give the okay, we'd appreciate it if you'd allow us to drill your well. We want to give our students some hands-on experience in well drilling."

Story 4: *How am I going to make this first month's Faith Promise?* an accountant wondered. He had recently relocated because of his job. He'd also attended a Faith Promise service a few days earlier at the church he planned to make his new church home and committed $100 a month to missions.

Although his new job would be a good one once he started work, it would be a few weeks before that happened. He'd had to take temporary work wherever he could find an employer who could use him for four or five weeks.

He found work, parking cars at a posh golf course.

One day while he was parking cars, a golfer pulled into the lot, jumped out of his Jaguar, and motioned for the brother to park it. The golfer slipped a tip to the brother, who just tucked it into his shirt pocket and promptly forgot about it.

After arriving home, he remembered the tip. Pulling it from his shirt pocket, he stared with surprise at a $100 bill.

Wow! he thought. *Here's my first month's Faith Promise!*

Story 5: While attending the Foreign Missions service at a general conference, a college girl made a commitment of $1,000. She did not know how she would be able to pay it, but God miraculously provided. A year and a half later she was in a Faith Promise service and felt directed to make a Faith Promise of $100 a month. She had already stepped out in faith once, and God had not failed her.

Two weeks later her phone rang.

"How are you doing, dear?" her caller asked.

"I'm doing just great!" the student replied as she recognized the voice of a lady from her church.

"Well, I am very happy for that," the woman said. "I called to tell you that I feel impressed to give you a hundred dollars a month."

The caller had to hold the phone away from her ear at the college girl's piercing scream of joy.

Story 6: A pastor bought a Laundromat, thinking it would be a good business to augment his income after he retired. To his disappointment, he found that the anticipated supplement to his income never materialized. In fact, the Laundromat produced very little profit. Then God spoke to the pastor that he was to send $500 a month for a foreign missions' project overseas.

The pastor did as he believed God directed him to do. He mailed $500 to foreign missions, planning to send $500 every month. After the pastor paid the first month's Faith Promise, however, his business sailed skyward like a stone from David's sling! The first month after keeping his Faith Promise, his profit from the Laundromat soared by $2000 a month! When he checked around to see what had caused the tremendous surge in profits, he discovered that a nearby Laundromat had gone out of business and the patrons started coming to his Laundromat!

Jack received a remarkable testimony from a married woman who had no job. She had made a Faith Promise of $25 a month and had been praying that the Lord would supply the means for her to honor her commitment. She and her husband conduct marriage retreats, but he is the one who gets paid! While she and her husband were holding a retreat for couples, she was asked to speak to the youth group. She obliged, not realizing until later that the Lord had used the retreat to enable her to give her foreign missions offering. She received an unexpected offering of—you guessed it!—$300, the exact amount she needed for her whole year's Faith Promise.

The promise was for a thousand dollars a month, not one hundred.

A pastor received an extremely interesting Faith Promise card signed by a couple in his church. *Hmmm,* he thought. *This family has committed nearly a hundred dollars a month to missions.* Then he looked at the card again. The promise was for a thousand dollars a month, not a thousand dollars a year.

Then, two months later, the husband walked out on his wife. To the pastor's surprise, the woman continued to meet the Faith Promise she and her husband had made together. Finally the pastor drew her aside.

"How are you able to give so much each month to missions?" he asked.

The woman shook her head. "Pastor," she said, "I work for an insurance company. After I made that commitment, business just started rolling in my direction. Isn't it wonderful? It's just the blessings of the Lord!"

For who has known the mind of the Lord? Or who has become His counselor? **(Romans 11:34, NKJV).**

Time and again, Jack was reminded that the Lord thinks far differently than we do. An elderly gentleman from the Lancaster, Ohio, church when Jack pastored there had been injured on the job and was waiting for a settlement. In a Faith Promise service, he determined that he was going to give all the settlement to missions. Not knowing what the settlement would be, he wrote on his Faith Promise card, "It's a secret." His gift of love was a real sacrifice because he lived in the country and did not have running water or a bathroom in the house. Having only the outside path to an outhouse, he could justifiably have used the money to make his life a bit more comfortable, but he obeyed what he felt the Lord wanted him to commit.

The settlement arrived, and the man kept his promise. He gave every cent of it to missions.

Then he fell ill. Although he was prayed for a number of times, he was not healed. In fact, a few months later he died.

Jack, being the man's pastor, was disturbed that the Lord had not healed the man.

"He gave so sacrificially," Jack mourned his friend to another minister. "I just believed the Lord would heal him."

"Your friend sent his offering on ahead," the other minister replied.

A district Foreign Missions director was attending a general conference and was given a check for $663 to help cover his trip expenses. In the Foreign Missions service he felt the Lord impress him to put that check in the offering.

Lord, is this really Your voice I'm hearing? he wondered. *You know we have a bill of twelve hundred dollars due. This check will pay for more than half of that bill!*

The impression to give the whole check flooded over him again, but still he hesitated. The unpaid bill that he owed loomed like a Goliath in his mind.

The offering plate neared the end of the row where he was sitting. Taking a deep breath, he hastily endorsed the check and dropped it in the offering plate as it passed him.

The following week he received an envelope from a minister he hardly knew. From the envelope he pulled out a note wrapped around a check for $500. "I feel I should send this to you," the note said.

Two weeks later he received another check for $2,500 from yet a different pastor.

Three thousand dollars! He'd given what was in his hand, and the Lord returned it nearly fivefold.

Two other very touching testimonies reminded Jack that a person's love offering to the Lord isn't always money, but the Lord sees the effort and love behind an outpouring of time and work.

A boy often shoveled snow and swept the walks for the widow of his former pastor.

"Let me pay you," she would always say.

Smiling, he always answered, "Put the money in the

missionary offering."

Years later, after the young boy had grown to be a man, the Lord called him to be a missionary. He was going on the Associates in Missions program for a short-term assignment. In the course of his raising funds to live on while abroad, his travels brought him back to his home church. After the service, the widow for whom he had done so many little odd jobs came up to the outgoing missionary and slipped an envelope into his hand.

"You always told me to put the money in the missionary offering," she said. "Do you remember? Well, you are that missionary, and the money is for you."

The widow had tucked an offering of $1,500 inside the envelope.

A second illustration of God's looking on the intent of the heart is beautifully portrayed by the story of a small girl from the South who entered her Sunday school class clutching three little flowers.

"Teacher, do you think the missionary would like these? I knew the missionary was coming, and I wanted to give him something," she further explained.

"I'm sure the missionary loves flowers," the teacher murmured.

"I looked and looked, but I couldn't find any money for the missionary offering this morning," the child continued. "These were all I could find to give him."

"Then these flowers are very special, and I'm sure the missionary will think so, too," the teacher said, hugging the little one before turning to wipe a tear from the corner of her eye. The little girl's parents were not in the church, but the child faithfully rode the church bus to Sunday school even though she often looked as if she had gotten up and dressed herself. The teacher was so moved that she went to her pastor between Sunday school and morning worship and told him the child's story.

"Let me take the flowers to the platform and see if I

The teacher was so moved she told the pastor the little girl's story.

---

can get any money out of them for the missionaries," the pastor said.

Then he related the story to the congregation.

"Is there anyone here who would give five hundred dollars for these flowers?" the pastor asked.

To the pastor's delight, an unsaved man sitting near the back of the church stood up. And what he said thrilled the minister even more.

"I will give you one thousand dollars for those flowers," he declared.

Those three slightly wilted, love-given flowers brought heaven down to earth.

Before the evening service was over, that man was baptized in Jesus' name and filled with the Holy Ghost.

During a camp meeting in a northern state, a minister presented a special project costing $5,000 in the country of Burma. A pastor in the congregation struggled within himself, wanting to give to the need but, in mentally tallying up his church's finances, knew the money just wasn't there. He felt, however, that they had to be involved anyway, so he stood.

"Our church will take care of the whole project," he said, to his own surprise.

Now what have I gotten the church into? he wondered. *Where in the world did* **that** *commitment come from?*

The following Sunday morning, he confessed to his congregation what he had felt impressed to do.

"If any of you want to give to this project, just see me after church," he said.

After his message he looked beyond the pulpit and saw people lined up along the center aisle of the church to tell him how much they would give.

Their offering exceeded $7,500.

The husbands and wives connection . . .

A Minnesota couple surprised each other when they returned to their home following a Faith Promise service.

Earlier that evening, he had been sitting on one side of the church.

She had been sitting on the other side of the building.

When the Faith Promise cards were to be signed, the husband thought he was supposed to make the commitment, and signed up for $50 a month.

His wife thought she was to make the Faith Promise, and signed up for $50 a month.

Each learned about their spouse's commitment when

they arrived home.

"Now what should we do?" they asked each other. "That means a Faith Promise of one hundred dollars a month instead of fifty dollars a month."

But they had both heard Jack preach Luke 6:38 in which Jesus said, "Give, and it shall be given unto you."

"Let's try God for the full amount," they decided.

The husband owned a delivery service where he delivered for several other companies. They decided to use the income from the smallest delivery to meet their Faith Promise. Within a short time, the small delivery service outgrew all his other deliveries. That took care of the amount on his Faith Promise card.

She worked for a nursing home, and within a few weeks she learned that she'd been promoted to manager with a sizable pay increase. And that took care of hers.

A wife got a big surprise when she discovered her husband had made a Faith Promise.

"Now remember, honey, we're going to the Faith Promise service, but we're not going to commit anything," the young husband admonished his wife before church on Faith Promise night.

"All right," his wife agreed. "After all, you've worked at the same job for fifteen years and haven't had a single pay raise in all that time. Your salary now is exactly what it was all those years ago."

As the service went on, however, the man thought of all the ways that the Lord had blessed him. Even with the cost of living going up for fifteen years, he and his wife had been able to meet all their financial obligations in spite of the lack of increase in his wages.

By the grace of God, we've managed, he thought. *Maybe we can commit ten dollars a month. After all, if that small offering of ten dollars a month can help one soul come to know the Lord, any sacrifice we make will be worth it.*

So he signed a Faith Promise card for $10 a month.

By the time he had paid $90 toward his $120 commitment for the year, his salary had spiraled to $4,000 above the previous year's income, and he had three months to go before the year would be up! And his wife didn't mind at all that he hadn't kept his word about signing a Faith Promise card.

Then there is the story of the husband who hadn't wanted to add to their previous year's Faith Promise. Wearing a big smile, his wife reported that she thought her husband would be willing to increase their Faith Promise commitment the current year.

"Last year he didn't want to increase the amount of our Faith Promise," she said to Jack. "He was quite skeptical. Very reluctantly he agreed to increase it by five dollars a month.

"Brother Leaman, my husband is a fireman. He was injured on the job and had filed a claim against his insurance. Soon after the service in which he had promised an additional five dollars a month, the insurance company settled for ten thousand dollars!

"I don't think he'll be so reluctant this year to increase our Faith Promise."

In the early days of the Faith Promise concept, missionaries went to the foreign field with very little guaranteed support. Nevertheless, they persevered, and God, not surprisingly, lavishly blessed their efforts for souls. Jack received this letter, with permission to use it, from Sister Martha Dobyns, who, with her husband Don, was a missionary appointed to Samoa in 1971, just two years after Faith Promise was introduced to the fellowship.

Dear Brother Leaman,

When we were appointed as missionaries in 1971, we had three personal Partners in Missions. Brother Box asked us if we wanted to cancel them, since we would be going into a very different circumstance. We had not even considered that. After a little thought, we told him we believed as long as God supplied we would give.

Many wonderful things happened. Once, a church of another denomination, in which we did

---

The money arrived the very day we needed exactly $50!

---

not know anyone, felt led to send us $500! Another time, the Lord woke up a senior in high school in the middle of the night and told him to send us $50. We had never met him. The money arrived the very day we needed exactly $50!

We were appointed to Samoa. Shortly after getting there, Brother Dobyns felt led to go to Fiji and Tonga, two neighboring countries. We asked Foreign Missions about it. There was no money allocated for [those countries] since we were not officially appointed to that area. But they gave us permission to go. So we used all the money we had gotten from the sale of our home and everything we could rake and scrape for Brother Dobyns to go as a tourist into those countries. We could not get a visa or work permit because our church was not registered there. He went as a tourist, not knowing one person in either country. God opened many doors.

After two years, we had ten congregations in Fiji and three in Tonga. Brother Dobyns was using half of our personal income to help the churches in these countries. At first I felt betrayed, but Brother Dobyns said, "Don't worry." And God did not fail us. The chief of our village sent enough meat every Sunday for our lunch, to last us all week. Once we needed $90 by the next day. Brother Dobyns went to the post office and came back empty-handed. No more mail for three days. About sundown a car drove into our yard. A lady got out and came in. The girls [our daughters] had met her in town. She said [they] had sold their old car for $700, and her unbelieving husband had told her to bring us the tithe. She had a check made out for $70 and laid it on the coffee table. She got up to go out the door, and it looked like a physical force caused her to turn around. She didn't say anything, just got her checkbook out and started to write. With tears streaming down her face, she handed me a check for $20 and said, "God told me to give this to you." We needed $90, not $70.

We were allowed to come to America for [general] conference after two years, providing we could pay our own way. We had used everything reaching into those new countries, even drew our ready reserve to the limit. God sent money from unexpected sources for us to go home to [general] conference. When we got there, Foreign Missions asked us to travel for three months to raise a budget for Tonga and Fiji. We had bought an old car to drive while at conference. A man tapped Brother Dobyns on the shoulder and asked him to trade cars with him. He was holding the keys to a brand-new Chevrolet Impala. He said, "This is your car for as long as you are in America."

When we came home for furlough, Brother Dobyns flew to Chicago to a Buick dealer. He let us buy a new Buick LeSabre for an unheard-of low price.

We went back overseas with four partners. We gave our all and after almost twenty years we came home with nothing, and God has given back to us more than we gave to Him! God is so wonderful. It is a privilege to live for the Lord.

Sincerely for Jesus,
Sister Martha Dobyns

God Is No Cheapskate

(. . . GOOD MEASURE . . .)

God is an incredible wheeler-dealer.

Really, He is.

In any swap meet with God, you always come out the winner.

You give Him your sins. He grants you salvation.

You present ashes. He bestows upon you the beauty of holiness.

You hand Him the filthy rags of your own righteousness. He imparts and imputes to you the righteousness of Jesus Christ.

You pile your burdens on Him. He willingly carries them for you and gives you rest.

Isaiah 60:17 records another trade-off: His gold for your bronze, His silver for your iron, His brass for your wood, and His iron for your stones.

Did you notice? God gets the short end of the stick in the exchange. Always.

God's Kind of Swap Meet

Would you trade $900 for $4,000? No, this was not a scam, nor was the $4,000 counterfeit. The result was a flat profit of $3,100, no strings attached. But a lot of questions had to be answered before the transaction took place.

The questions occupied the minds of a young college couple living on such a tight budget that if they squeezed it, it turned purple. He was in his final year of college, but where would the job be after he graduated? Would they have to move for him to find a good job? How could they afford to move? Shouldn't they be saving toward a move? If they moved, would they have to buy furniture?

Shouldn't the $75 a month they committed to their Faith Promise be tucked away in a savings account?

Taking stock, they buried their doubts and decided to trust the Lord that their questions would be answered in a few months. But the seed of faith they planted sprouted and bloomed much sooner than they dreamed.

Within the month, the university hired the young woman.

As a result, he got his tuition free.

He got a discount on his textbooks.

Their rent was reduced.

His parking fee cost less.

They calculated that her new job saved them over $4,000 for the upcoming term. Quite an uneven exchange for their $900 a year commitment to Faith Promise, wasn't it? God is no cheapskate when payback time rolls around.

Arkansas: A pastor in the Midwest experienced this lopsided receiving in a delightful way when one of the members of his church approached him.

"Pastor, I really wish you would trade in your old car," Bob pleaded. "That old clunker you're driving has over three hundred thousand miles on it. I'm afraid you'll never get to general conference if you drive there."

"Bob, I appreciate your concern," the pastor said. Then with a smile, because he did not want to offend so faithful a saint, he said, "I don't feel trading in the car is something I should do right now. We'll get to the conference; you'll see."

The pastor and his wife arrived safely at the conference and enjoyed the services, the meetings, and being with friends. During the Foreign Missions service, newly appointed missionaries were introduced.

"Let's take all ten of them on. After all, the car is still running."

With a thoughtful look on his face, the minister turned to his wife. "You know, if we take on all ten missionaries as personal Partners in Missions, that would be about the price of a car payment."

"Let's take all ten of them on," she agreed. "After all, the car is still running."

Rejoicing in the refreshing they had received at the conference, the couple returned home. Shortly afterward someone phoned the pastor at his home.

"Pastor, are you busy this afternoon? Fred and I'd like to stop by for a few minutes. I have something I want to give you."

Now what could that possibly be? the pastor wondered.

He soon found out! When he opened his door to his visitors, he saw a new Ford Explorer in his driveway.

His visitors grinned.

"This is what we want to give you," one of the brothers said.

Speechless, the pastor could only look at the men.

"Come on," the men urged. "Get in it! Look it over! It's yours."

On surprise-weakened legs, the pastor strode to the vehicle, opened its door, and slid behind the wheel.

"The instruction manual is in the glove compartment," his callers said, wide smiles and twinkling eyes indicating something else was in store for their pastor.

Still in shock, the pastor snapped open the glove compartment. Yes, there lay the instruction manual. But an envelope with his name on it peeked from under the manual.

Inside the envelope he found a wad of bills. His fingers trembling, he counted out $2,700!

He turned to his smiling benefactors.

"The money is to pay the taxes on the car," they explained.

Texas: A husband and wife from the South tried to swap their vacation for their Faith Promise commitment. Notice: tried to swap.

"Dear, how much do you think we should give to our Faith Promise?" a man asked his wife.

Without hesitation, she answered, "One hundred

dollars a month."

"That's a lot of money," her husband replied. "Maybe we shouldn't promise quite so much. Our van is going to have to be replaced soon."

"I know that's a lot of money and I know we have to do something about the poor old van," she admitted, "but I feel that is what we should give."

That night they turned in their commitment of $100 a month.

At daybreak the Lord woke up the woman's dad.

"Give your daughter and her husband a new van," the Lord impressed on the man's mind. So he did.

With a new van replacing their old, battered VW, the couple doubled their commitment, increasing it to $200 a month.

"The work of God is more important than our having a vacation."

"After all," the husband said, "God blessed us with the van. Let's double our Faith Promise. What do you think of our not taking a vacation this year? It would be easier to meet our foreign missions commitment if we stayed home."

His wife thought about that a minute. "The work of God is more important than our having a vacation," she agreed. "Besides, just think how much housework and yard work we can get done if we stay home!"

A few days later the man came home from work and

called to his wife. "You'll never guess what happened at work today!" he exclaimed.

"Tell me, tell me," the woman begged.

"We're going on vacation after all! The company is sending me to Los Angeles on a business trip, and you are going, too! All expenses paid! Round-trip airfare for both of us, hotel, food, spending money, vacation time—the works."

Afterward, they tallied up the worth of the vacation to be about $5,200. That was more than double their doubled Faith Promise!

Texas: A quite different exchange between a pastor, a missionary, and God occurred. Although the pastor had invited the missionary to present the need for his particular field of endeavor, he told the missionary that the church couldn't take him on as a Partner in Missions.

"Although the church can't help with your support, I want to be a Partner in Missions with you," the pastor said, "so I'll take you on personally for twenty-five dollars a month."

The pastor had applied for a loan on a new home, and it had been approved for a certain percentage rate. A short time after the minister had promised his personal support to the missionary, his loan was reapproved for one percent less. The monthly savings on the new loan—$100.

Examples of True Faith: Jobless People Commit to Faith Promise . . .

Indiana: A man who had no business—in fact, he was laid off from his job—felt that the Lord was talking to him to make a commitment of $85 a month.

"Now, wait a minute, Lord," he objected. "I'm laid off from my job. I don't want to promise You something and then not be able to keep my promise!"

The nudge from the Spirit persisted, however, so he filled out his Faith Promise card with $85 as his commitment.

Then, since he was only laid off, not lazy, he decided to put legs on his faith and went looking for another job.

He found one. It paid $20,000 more a year than his old job.

That's $1,666.67 a *month* more!

"I'm so thankful I obeyed the Lord," he declared.

So, the following year, he increased his giving to $210 a month, or $2,520 for the year.

Of course, the Lord honored the bigger basket of faith. He filled the man's basket with an unexpected bonus of $2,500 shortly afterward.

They bought stock in God's blue-chip firm.

Ohio: Any investment that paid ten times a month the cost of the stock would be considered an excellent risk. However, the risk this newly married couple faced was the possibility of the husband's losing his job. The firm he worked for teetered on the edge of bankruptcy.

In the first Faith Promise service he and his wife had ever attended, he questioned her on the amount she felt they should give.

"Fifty dollars a month," she whispered.

"Okay," he whispered back as he signed their Faith Promise card. "That's what I feel we should give, too."

Within the month, he found new employment paying $500 a month more than his old job.

"Brother Leaman, that's ten times a month what my monthly Faith Promise was," he related.

Then they realized that their commitment had been no risk at all because their stock was in the Lord, and God's blue-chip firm produces great dividends.

Ohio: After being unable to find a job to sustain herself while going to Bible school, a greatly disappointed young lady returned home. For six weeks she did everything she knew to do to find a job but to no avail. During a Faith Promise service at her church, she argued with God about the commitment she felt He was prompting her to make.

"How can I make a commitment for a monthly offering for foreign missions when I don't even have a job?" she questioned God.

She wanted to stay sensitive to the Spirit, however, so she marked the amount she felt the Lord was talking to her about and turned in her Faith Promise card.

The following Tuesday the phone company called.

"We don't have any part-time jobs at this time," she was told. "Would you accept an offer for a full-time job?"

Would she ever!

Tennessee: To many folks, a Faith Promise of $25 a month would seem quite conservative, but to a single mom with three small children, no job, and fitful child support, such a step took a lot of faith.

That faith was sorely tried when Susan blew a tire on

70

her car. A new tire cost $100, and she simply didn't have the money to buy it.

Then she received a letter in the mail.

"Do you remember all those clothes you gave us several years ago?" a friend wrote. "I never did pay you for them although I always wanted to. Here's one hundred dollars for the clothes. I'm sorry it took so long!"

The woman rejoiced over the check because she would be able to pay for a new tire and went to the tire store to purchase it.

"I know the old tire won't be covered by the warranty," she told the store manager, "but God sent me this money so I'm going to be okay."

The salesman grabbed the phone, made some quick calls, and got the blown-out tire covered anyway.

In one week Susan had received her Faith Promise, a new tire, and money to carry them through a non-payment of child support crisis.

Kentucky: An enterprising, stay-at-home mom was a Certified Nurse's Assistant. A new convert, she knew virtually nothing about the Lord and His Word. Nevertheless, she felt impressed to make a Faith Promise of $125 a month.

At the end of the service, the pastor drew her aside.

"Sister, do you understand that your Faith Promise can be a monthly or weekly commitment?" he asked.

"Yes, Pastor," she replied. "I am aware of that, and my commitment is $125 a month."

She went home and told her husband what she had done. Her husband had never made a move for the Lord, but he was very supportive in tithing and stated that he understood the "blessing and curse thing" that the Bible speaks of in the area of finances. Still, he had questions.

"How do you expect us to be able to pay that?" he asked.

"I'll work for it," she replied.

"Do you really think you can make that kind of money staying at home?" he asked with a great deal of skepticism.

"God will help me," she responded, confident in her newly found faith.

"Good luck, then," he said, shrugging his shoulders.

Before long, and without advertising, she had three phone calls from different families needing someone to sit part-time with an elderly parent or grandparent. She discussed fees with her callers, and when she tallied her figures, she realized she would be earning a starting weekly salary of $280.

"Just think," she exclaimed. "In only one week I'll make twice the amount of my monthly Faith Promise!"

Needle and bread help a clever woman keep her Promise.

Minnesota: Another resourceful woman used her expertise at sewing to meet her Faith Promise increase of $50 a month, and a neighbor unwittingly helped her do it. He asked her if she would mend three pairs of trousers that he had.

"I'll pay you fifteen dollars to fix each pair," he told her.

In her mind, the lady was thinking, *That's forty-five*

of the fifty dollars I need to meet this month's Faith Promise. Thank You, Lord!

When the gentleman came to pick up the neatly mended trousers, he took $45 from his wallet. As he handed her the money, he hesitated.

Oh, dear! the lady thought. *Didn't I do a good enough job?*

Aloud she asked, "Is there something wrong?"

"Oh, no! No! The pants are fine! They look great! But I was just wondering, since I live so close and I drive right past your house on my way to work, would you pack a nice lunch for me every day? Would five dollars a lunch be enough?"

The woman thought quickly: *Five dollars a day with twenty workdays a month equals one hundred dollars a month! That's enough to pay my Faith Promise each month and buy the food for his lunches.*

"That would be fine," the woman agreed with a smile. "I'll make the lunches as interesting and as tasty as I can."

"If they taste as good as these pants look, I'll be pleased," the man said as he left her house. "Good-bye for now, and thank you."

"And thank You, Lord," the woman whispered as she shut the door. She had never dreamed that help could be as close as her neighbor!

"Bear ye one another's burdens . . .

. . . and so fulfil the law of Christ," states Galatians 6:2. A saint in **Mississippi** did just that by assuming an elderly couple's Faith Promise!

"Pastor, I'd like to pay the Dunwoodys' Faith Promise for the whole year. I know they are on a fixed income and are just scraping by." The man grinned. "Let's keep this a secret just between you and me. It'll be fun to be a blessing to those dear old folks. They've been an inspiration to me, just thinking of all the years they've served God so faithfully."

"They are an inspiration to the whole church," the pastor agreed. "This is a good thing you are doing, Mack."

The next Sunday, the pastor noticed a wide, crescent smile on Mack's face. So after service as he shook Mack's hand, he murmured, "Mack, you look like the proverbial cat that caught the canary."

"I did," Mack replied softly. "Pastor, three days after I took on the Dunwoodys' Faith Promise, I received an unexpected check in the mail. It was made out for three times the amount of their entire year's Faith Promise!"

Georgia: In the neighboring state of Georgia, another couple took Mack's act of faith a step further and assumed a missions commitment for their whole church. While attending a general conference, the pair heard their pastor commit their congregation to $5,000 for overseas literature in the Foreign Missions service and $2,500 in the Home Missions service. On the way home, they decided to pay the total amount their pastor had promised and that they should pay it for the church. They had two pieces of property they had been trying to sell for several months. The month they paid the $7,500 for the church they sold both pieces of property and made $75,000 profit from the sales.

From **Maryland** comes the case of the mystified missionary.

This is a switch from the ordinary, thought Jack as he read about an unusual twist to the normal operation of things. *A missionary on deputation giving an offering to a home missions pastor?*

That was quite a swap!

God spoke to a missionary to give the pastor an offering. The missionary had many needs of his own besides raising funds to return to the mission field, but he knew he had heard from the Lord. He obeyed the Lord and gave the pastor an offering. Then he and his wife drove off in a battered, old car with their possessions strapped to a rack on top.

Later that week the missionary preached in another church. After the service, the pastor led him to his study.

"Brother, please wait here until we call for you," the pastor requested of the mystified missionary.

A short time later, the pastor led him through the foyer of the church to the driveway outside. A fine motor home sat parked in the driveway.

"This is yours to use until you have finished your deputation," the pastor said, handing the keys to the vehicle to an astonished missionary.

The missionary looked back to the previous service and was glad he had obeyed the Lord in giving the home missionary pastor an offering.

That was quite a swap, Jack thought. *The missionary's offering to the home missionary was way out of proportion to the benefits he received from being able to use the motor home for the next several months.*

Are You Thinking with Your Head . . .

Texas: Across the continent, a woman was having nightmares over the Faith Promise commitment she and her husband had made earlier that evening. She had felt fine while they were at church and she was glad they had made a commitment, but she worried about the amount and confessed as much to her husband on their way home from church.

"Do you think we promised too much?" Nick had asked.

"Do you think we truly heard from the Lord when we put down the figure? We have so many bills. Maybe we were being foolish. Maybe we just got carried away by the spirit of giving that was in the service."

"We'll wait and see," Nick had responded.

Nick's answer didn't lessen Sue's worry. In bed, she tucked the pillow under her cheek and closed her eyes. As soon as she did that, the amount of their electric bill popped up like a jack-in-the-box against her closed eyelids. She rolled onto her back and opened her eyes. Light filtering in from a streetlight on the corner lit the ceiling to smoky grayness, and Sue thought about the repair bill they'd had for the washing machine. She curled onto her left side and saw her husband's broad, sheet-draped shoulder with the phone bill superimposed on it. She blinked to erase the mental picture. Thinking about the money they had promised to missions and calculating their bills, she started to panic.

At last she told the Lord that they'd just trust they had really heard from Him, and she put the matter out of her mind and fell asleep.

On Tuesday, the manager called her into his office for a meeting with him and her supervisor.

"Sue, a lot of people have been leaving the company for higher salaries elsewhere," her manager said.

"Our employee survey indicates that employees are very dissatisfied with their salaries," the supervisor said.

Sue had recently received her second raise in six months and was very satisfied with her salary. However, before she got a chance to say so, her manager continued the conversation.

"The company has evaluated everyone's salaries, Sue," he said.

"You are going to receive a twenty-four percent raise," the supervisor concluded.

Dazed by the unexpected news and stunned by the amount of the increase in her salary, Sue sort of wobbled down the hall toward her office. The raise was twice the amount of their year's Faith Promise.

Michigan: George, a car salesman, had made a Faith Promise during the previous year's missions' conference. Then he started thinking with his head and did not pay it. The Lord gently nagged him about paying up. George brushed it aside. Finally, the Lord dealt so strongly with George that he paid the whole year's Faith Promise with the full amount: $240. Although George had procrastinated almost to the point of disobedience, God did not delay in responding to George. Within two weeks of writing his check to missions, George received an unexpected check from the Chrysler Corporation for $280 for outstanding salesmanship.

Although George had procrastinated almost to the point of disobedience, God did not delay in responding to George.

Texas: Sally's young husband had become embittered and refused to come to church with her. He had replaced going to church with joyrides on his motorcycle. He had no job, and she was making his monthly motorcycle payment of $147 on her salary of $17,000 per year. At the Faith Promise service, she told the Lord that she was committing the same amount to missions that she paid on the motorcycle. Her husband was not too happy about that! Soon thereafter, the husband left his wife. Some of the last words he flung at her were, "Now see what your God can do for you!"

This sweet, early-twenty-year-old saint with only a high school education began to see the blessings of God on her finances. Within a few short months she was earning $37,000 per year. She raised her Faith Promise accordingly. A few days later she informed her pastor that she had been approached by a headhunter and had been offered a high paying job.

That first year, her salary jumped to $120,000. The

next year, she earned more than $150,000, and her income continued to grow. Then the head thinking took over. She chose to no longer give to missions and in time left the church. Today she is making good money; however, with two divorces and a child born out of wedlock, she has long since lost the joy of her blessing.

She could not figure out in her human mind how she would be able to keep her commitment.

Washington: As a Foreign Missions conference approached, a lady found herself pondering how much she would be able to commit. About a week earlier, the Human Resources personnel at her job had explained that for two and a half years an error had been made on her paycheck and she had not been paid accurately. They gave her a check for the difference, and she thought this solved her Faith Promise puzzle.

Then commitment night came. She calculated what the check from her work would average per month and started to fill out her card with that amount.

The Lord kept dealing with her about a greater amount, an amount more than she had thought to commit. She struggled throughout the service, not wanting to accept what God was saying to her. She could not figure out in her human mind how she would be able to do it. However, at the last minute she nervously signed the card with the amount the Lord had impressed her to commit.

The next day at work, Human Resources came to her and surprised her again.

"We're sorry, but we've made another mistake," she was told. "The check we gave you last week was not enough. Here is the rest of the amount you should have been paid."

They presented her with another check. That check, coupled with the previous one, enabled her to triple her Faith Promise commitment over what it had been the previous year. So although she started out thinking with her head, she ended up thinking with her heart.

. . . Or Are You Thinking with Your Heart?

Money means very little to God. After all, He owns the cattle on a thousand hills! The earth is the Lord's, and the fullness thereof. And that shiny metal stuff that man digs out of the dirt and covets and lies for and cheats for and kills to get is only pavement in heaven! The giver's attitude matters greatly to God.

Jack's files bulge with stories of God's people who ignored "head thinking" with its reasoning, rationalizing, and analyzing. Instead, these saints' hearts led them to heed Paul's injunction in II Corinthians 9:7: "Every man according as he purposeth in his heart, so let him give; not grudgingly, or of necessity: for God loveth a cheerful giver."

Leaman smiles at the report of a Florida church where the members, when it is time to take the offering, clap and cheer because God has blessed them so much and has given them the opportunity to give back to Him.

Indiana: An unsaved businessman startled the pastor of the church his wife attended.

"I'll match all the other Faith Promise commitments made by members in the church," he promised. "Add them up and let me know how much the total is."

The man kept his promise, enabling the church to double its commitment to foreign missions. A year later, he heard a missionary from Liberia express a need for a Bible school building.

"The building will cost eighty thousand dollars," the missionary stated.

After the service, the businessman told the pastor that he would pay for the school building. "I'll pay half this year and the other half next year," he promised.

Well, his business flourished to the point where other businessmen noticed how he prospered.

"Come on, tell us your secret," they implored him. "What are you doing to help your business grow?"

"Giving to missions," the man replied. "Ever since I started giving to missions, my business has just exploded! Give to God's cause, and He will bless your business, too!"

Ohio: "Lord, what should my Faith Promise be?" a man questioned the Lord.

Ralph felt that the Lord was leading him to make a $300 a month commitment, so that's what he penned on his card before he turned it in.

The pastor pulled Ralph aside after service. "Man, you shouldn't make that size of a commitment," the pastor exclaimed. "You only make two hundred dollars a week on your mechanic's job, and your tithe is eighty dollars a month. By promising this much to foreign missions, you'll be living on only half your income!"

"Pastor, there are a lot of things I cannot do in the church, but this I can do," the man explained.

Still concerned, the pastor watched the missionary offering that month and noticed that Ralph's money showed up.

"Pastor, there are many things I cannot do in the church, but this I can do."

The $300 appeared the second month, too.

Sometime during the third month following the Faith Promise service, the fellow was called into his boss's office.

"Ralph, I'm going to open another garage in the city. I want you to manage it. I need a man I can trust. You are very skilled and utterly dependable. Would you consider managing the new garage?" the boss asked.

Shocked numb and dumb, Ralph could only stare at his boss. "Well . . . I, um . . . er. . . ."

"By the way," the boss continued, "I pay my managers $800 a week."

With a huge grin, Ralph accepted the increased responsibilities of running the new shop profitably and honestly. But he was thinking, *Wow! I'll be earning in one week what I used to work a whole month for!*

Of course his tithes increased, too.

And an overcautious pastor learned a lesson in faith.

Tennessee: A businessman owned a small business when he made his first Faith Promise for $50 a month. He faithfully tucked a check for foreign missions in the offering every month.

The next year, finding that God had prospered him, he doubled his Faith Promise to $100 a month. As before, he was able to meet his commitment.

His third commitment doubled his second one so that he was putting $200 a month, or $50 a week into missions.

On his fourth year of giving to foreign missions, he doubled the third year's commitment so that he was giving $400 a month, or $100 a week.

God continued to bless until he was able to send $500 a week to help the church he attended support even more Partners in Missions.

Now, that kind of giving caught the attention of the man's pastor, who went to the man and asked how he could give $26,000 a year to Faith Promise.

The man's answer was a classic. "Well," he said, "my business just keeps growing, so I just keep giving."

Missouri: *The raise I'm expecting will be nice,* a man thought as he pondered the amount to write on his Faith Promise card. *But the Lord has enabled us to live fine on the salary I'm making now, so I'll just give the whole amount of the raise to Him.*

A month went by. When the man opened the envelope of his paycheck, he smiled, anticipating a nice increase behind the dollar sign.

It wasn't there. The raise hadn't come through.

The man was faithful to his commitment, however, even

though it meant scrimping a bit throughout the month.

It doesn't matter, he thought, still cheerful. *The raise will come through next month.*

But it didn't. Again, the man watched his expenditures closely so that he could keep his promise made by faith.

The anticipated raise had not come through.

The third month the raise came through. The man looked with disbelief at the figures on the check. The raise was five times what he had expected it to be!

Ohio: Wouldn't you think that a young couple that had filed a Chapter 13 bankruptcy would know better than to commit themselves to added debt? When someone is in such financial straits that they have to file for bankruptcy and show they don't have enough money to pay their bills, wouldn't you think their thinking skewed if they committed $50 a month to Faith Promise? And wouldn't you believe they had fallen over the edge when they doubled that amount for the next year?

Yet a young couple did just that because they thought with their hearts. The young man's dad had died some months earlier, and the inheritance had been tied up. Within the month of the couple's making their Faith Promise, the estate was settled and he received one-half his inheritance of $8,000. He was able to pay his year's Faith Promise that very month.

Ohio: "All these wonderful things happened because

we stepped out in faith," enthused another young couple. Their wedding was only a few weeks away, but their minds were truly married when they agreed on a commitment to foreign missions for $200 a month.

The very next day after they signed a Faith Promise card, the young man received a hefty pay raise of $10,000 a year! And within the same month, they found a very nice apartment at unbelievably low rent.

Oklahoma: "Brother Leaman, I'd like to tell you how the Lord helped me and my husband in making our Faith Promise," an excited lady bubbled to Jack after a Faith Promise service.

"Earlier today I prayed and asked the Lord what our family should give. I felt impressed that we should commit five hundred dollars for the coming year. Then I prayed several more times today because we do not have much money to live on. Finally I told the Lord that He would have to talk to my husband since he was the head of the house.

"Tonight in the service I was sitting next to him, watching to see what amount he wrote on the card. Brother Leaman, I had not told him what I had felt we should do. Do you know what? He wrote down ten dollars a week! I'm so excited because that is a little more than what I felt to commit. Isn't the Lord wonderful?"

Jack talked to the pastor several months later and asked him if that couple had been able to pay their commitment.

"Yes, they've been very faithful to keep their Faith Promise," the pastor replied. "The man has received several raises since that service, and the last raise was a dollar eighty an hour."

Jack did some quick figuring. That one raise alone earned the man a profit of $248 a month over his Faith Promise commitment.

That one raise alone earned the man a profit of $248 a month above his Faith Promise commitment.

Tennessee: Joe's fourteen hours of work manning the front desk each week at the local YMCA coupled with his small pension provided barely adequate funds for him and his wife to live on. A former police officer, he had been injured while making an arrest and subsequently became disabled. Before their church's Faith Promise service, they agreed to leave their Faith Promise the same as the year before.

During the service, however, they both felt that they should increase it 150 percent. "Lord, if we are going to be able to meet this commitment, I need an answer from You," he prayed.

They struggled to pay the first month's commitment, but they faithfully kept their promise to the Lord.

Not long afterward, his hours on his job were raised to thirty a week, which represented about eight times per month what his Faith Promise was.

Indiana: In order to pay her first month's Faith

Promise of $50, a pastor's daughter scraped together all her extra dimes, nickels, and pennies to do so. Within a couple of weeks, however, she realized a sizeable profit on the sale of a home she had tried to sell for several months with hardly any offer. Within this same time period, as she continued to give to God faithfully in tithes, offerings, and her other commitments, she received not only a promotion but also two separate raises at work that equaled over $5,000.

Florida: A young lady planned to go to Spain on the Associates in Missions program. She had a car note that amounted to $326 a month and knew that she could not go unless that car note was taken care of.

In a Faith Promise service she felt impressed to make a $25 a month commitment, but concern over that car note still plagued her. She presented the problem to the Lord, and that very day a friend agreed to make the car payment while she was gone.

That young lady embarked for Spain from the West Palm Beach, Florida, church, whose pastor, Brother Daniel Kyle, wrote the following letter to Jack.

> I count it a great privilege to be able to write and tell of the wonderful things that God has done for the Tabernacle of Pentecost in West Palm Beach, Florida. When my family and I came to West Palm Beach thirteen years ago, the church was supporting just a few missionaries, but today with the help of God, we now support well over one hundred missionaries! We have

also helped to build churches and colleges in foreign countries.

I link this growth directly to our Faith Promise services. Initially, I was very hesitant to have our first Faith Promise service. I felt insecure and was concerned that the extra giving of monies to foreign missions would rob from other pertinent places in our budget where the money was of an

I was very hesitant
to have our first Faith Promise service.

absolute necessity. However, I quickly came to find out that when people begin to give to foreign missions it opens up their heart to give even more abundantly in all other areas. The numerous blessings that were received by individual families of the church as a result of their giving are so abundant it would take pages to tell them all.

God has increased our church in many ways. In a recent meeting with our banker, he suggested that we cease from giving large amounts of monies to foreign missions in order to better afford our building project. I informed him that it was because of our giving to foreign missions that we were able to afford to build in the first place. It was just three days after taking that stand that a brother donated $300,000 to the building program!

I believe when we put God's kingdom first and sacrifice to reach others around the world, He will abundantly bless us right here at home. There is no quicker way to seeing your needs met than that of meeting the needs of others.

Between Rocks and Other Hard Places

(. . . PRESSED DOWN . . .)

Have you ever experienced the agony of being squeezed between a rock and a hard place? In one Colorado family, being between a rock and a hard place meant deciding which bill to pay, but oh, what a pressed-down blessing they received when they chose God over mammon!

"What shall we do this month?" a man asked his wife. "Shall we pay our Faith Promise and be short on our rent, or shall we pay the rent and let some of the Faith Promise slide until next month?"

His wife looked at him as if he were speaking Swahili. "We pay our Faith Promise, of course," she insisted.

So they paid their $100 Faith Promise for December.

"We can pay only part of our rent," the husband reminded his wife.

"How much is part?" his wife asked.

"We can pay $150 of it," he replied.

"That means we'll still be behind $350," the woman sighed.

"I think if we explain to the landlord that we can pay a third of our rent and promise him the rest as soon as we can, he'll consent to that." And picking up the phone, the husband called the landlord and explained the problem.

"We'll pay the balance as soon as we receive it," the husband assured his landlord.

"Bring the $150 over to me," the landlord said.

When the man arrived he gave the landlord the $150. The landlord sat and wrote a receipt for $500—the amount of the rent—and handed it to the man.

Then he presented the $150 to him, too.

"Merry Christmas," the landlord said with a smile.

The Lord made us
better money managers.

A Southern family on food stamps heard Jack preach on Faith Promise. They made their commitment that night as the Lord directed.

"The following services we heard many testify about the financial blessings that they were receiving," the wife in the family later testified. "But our family did not see any financial miracle happen. It wasn't until the end of the year that we realized what the Lord had done for us. Instead of the Lord blessing us with financial miracles, we discovered that He had made us better money managers!"

Even though this **Minnesota** church had partici-
pated enthusiastically in Faith Promise for many years,
things were not going well. A deep downturn in the econ-
omy of the whole region forced people to leave the area.
A number of families had left the church for this reason.
Their exodus affected both the general income of the
church and the missionary offering.

The pastor was concerned that he would have to
choose between the rock of paying the church's
Partners in Missions commitment or the hard place of
paying the mortgage!

The pastor's fears never materialized. The church
had been able to send in their Faith Promise commitment
every month.

How could this be happening? the pastor wondered.

He scrutinized the church financial records. Over
the same time span, the interest rate on the church's
mortgage kept going down and down, so the church
payment became less and less. One day it dawned on
the pastor to see how much his church payment had
been reduced. To his amazement, it had gone down
several hundred dollars.

The lower bank payment let them maintain their level
of foreign missions giving!

A doctor in **Tennessee** pledged $10,050 to the
building fund. God restored this amount through a tax
refund within forty-eight hours. He and his wife had
anticipated *paying* income taxes. The following week
they made a Faith Promise monthly commitment of
$250. God blessed him with unexpected income of

$30,000 through speaking fees from medical lectures. A tenfold return can surely be counted as a pressed-down blessing, can't it?

A Midwestern pastor in his first Faith Promise service thought that he would take a baby step and commit $5 a month.

Then God spoke to him. "Make that $35 a month."

The pastor was on a very tight budget but "Nevertheless at Thy word . . ." obeyed the Lord. Within the month he received a raise.

The following year's Faith Promise challenged him again, and once more the Lord gave direction.

This time God said, "Make that $75."

He did, and within two weeks the pastor received another raise.

The third year God said, "Double the $75 a month to $150 a month."

Whoa, Nellie! The pastor started complaining to God because many in his congregation weren't giving. That year he struggled to pay his commitment.

Eventually he felt the call of God to the mission field, applied, and was appointed. While on deputation he wasn't doing very well raising his support.

"Why, God?" he asked one day while praying. "I'm answering Your call."

Then the Lord impressed him to increase his percent of giving. As soon as he obeyed, the offerings he received increased noticeably.

Between More Rocks and More Hard Places . . .

Consider this scattering of "between a rock and a hard place" testimonies, where people, pinched by finances, responded to Faith Promise anyway, and, in turn, experienced "pressed down" blessings from the Lord:

An **Ohio** couple made a Faith Promise during the missionary conference at their church. The wife had been married before, and her former husband had left the state, moved to Florida, and was welshing on child support payments. They had given up on receiving alimony, but after they declared their Faith Promise, they received a letter from the State of Florida and began receiving regular, monthly child support.

A working pastor in **Tennessee** assumed Partners in Missions support for the five missionaries who were presented at a "Because of the Times" conference. Three months later his salary was doubled.

A retiree in **Ohio** who had belonged to the carpenters' union increased his Faith Promise of $50 a month to $350 a month. The following week he received word that his yearly raise, instead of being the normal 3 percent, would be 10 percent. In addition, the raise would be retroactive to January of that year. That paid his whole year's Faith Promise increase.

A young man in **Colorado** made a $25 a month Faith Promise although his checking account was as deflated as a pricked balloon. That same month he started a business and grossed $6,300 the first month. He has been going strong every since.

As the offering was being taken during the Foreign Missions service at a **general conference**, a lady walked to a nearby microphone and stated that she was giving her wedding ring because she had nothing else to give. Two men standing by told her to keep her ring, and each man replaced her ring with $50.

One missionary during **School of Missions** increased his own Partner in Missions commitment by $150 per month. The following Sunday the missionary received a $2,000 offering that paid not only his personal, yearly Partners in Missions increase but also his tithes.

A retired man in **Ohio** who had worked for the Ford Motor Company for over thirty years made a $60 a month Faith Promise while wondering how he could pay it. Within the month he received a notice from the Ford Motor Company that all former employees with thirty years of service would receive a $60 a month increase in their pension.

A finish carpenter in **Florida** in a vise financially made his first Faith Promise of $30 a month. Five days later he was blessed with a tremendous schedule of work installing trim on 140 two- and three-bedroom apartment units. That job guaranteed him work for the next six to twelve months, and maybe longer.

A lady in **Indiana** made a Faith Promise of $10 a month. She had loaned someone $5,000 before she was married and did not expect to get it back. After she made her Faith Promise, she received the money she had loaned.

A **Tennessee** couple made a Faith Promise on

Sunday night despite squeezed finances. The woman recently had been laid off from her job at the telephone company. Monday morning the company called her back to work.

She was so excited that she phoned her husband at his work. Unfortunately, his line was busy.

Disappointed, she hung up the phone, only to have it buzz under her hand. She grabbed it up and heard her husband's voice.

"I just tried to call you," the woman said. "I have fantastic news. The phone company called me back to work!"

"My phone was busy because I was trying to call you," her husband explained. "I just got a raise!"

An **Ohio** homemaker felt the Lord direct her to make a Faith Promise of $40 a month, knowing she would have to wring it out of her housing allowance. A few weeks later she received a check from her uncle. "Dear Niece," the accompanying note read, "I cashed in some stocks when the market was high. I want to share some of the profits with you." He had enclosed a check for $10,000.

The Peter, James, and John Fishing Company had been fishing all night and had caught nothing. Tired, dirty, hungry, discouraged, and smelly, they dragged their boats ashore and spread out their nets to dry. Jesus strolled by and asked Peter if He could borrow his boat for a while. After using the boat as a pulpit, Jesus paid the three fishermen for the use of their boat in an unusual way.

"Row out into deep water and let down your nets for a huge catch," He told them.

Well, now. Any real fisherman knew that in the Sea of Galilee, fish were caught at night in shallow water, not in the daytime in deep water. Jesus asked Peter to do something contrary to all his training and experience.

Maybe Peter shrugged his shoulders. Maybe he thought he should tell Him that they had already fished all night and caught zilch. Maybe he should educate Jesus on fishing because, after all, Jesus had been raised inland in a carpenter's shop, so what did He know about fishing? Maybe he opened his mouth to protest and then snapped it shut when he remembered that Jesus had healed Peter's mother-in-law. Maybe. What he did was reply, "Nevertheless at thy word I will let down the net."

So Peter let down one net. But the Lord had said, "Nets." Plural. More than one net.

The one net that Peter let down couldn't support the weight of the resulting catch. The pressed-down blessing broke the net. The fish escaped back into the sea. Peter yelled for help.

Fortunately, James and John heard Peter holler and saw his frantically windmilling arms. They rowed to his aid, let down their nets, and heaved up enough fish to nearly swamp both boats and threaten to dump them all into the lake.

But it made a believer out of Peter. He fell to Jesus' feet, wallowed around in the mess of slippery fish, confessed his sinfulness of unbelief, and called Jesus "Lord." You see, Jesus still sat in the filled-to-the-gunwales boat.

Jesus was in the proverbial boat to bless a modern-day

angler from Florida who stepped out in faith just as Peter had. Actually, the man was a fishing guide who had made a substantial Faith Promise of $1,000 a month. Being a professional fisherman, he decided to participate in a bass tournament.

He phoned a potential sponsor. "Hey, Tom! I'm going to enter the bass fishing tournament, and I'm wondering if you'd sponsor me for five thousand dollars?"

"Five thousand?" his friend roared. "Man, I'm going to sponsor you for twenty-five thousand dollars."

And just like that, his $12,000 commitment was satisfied.

In seeking God for an answer as to why he had not yet received the Holy Ghost, it occurred to a boat owner in Michigan that maybe he loved his boat too much. *I'll just sell the boat*, he thought. *Then maybe the Lord will see the sincerity of my heart and fill me with the Holy Ghost.*

He advertised and tried to sell the boat at a ridiculously low price, but no one answered his ads. Now that he couldn't sell the boat, he needed an anchor. The anchor he wanted cost $100.

When his $100 a month Faith Promise fell due, he debated: Should he buy the anchor or pay his Faith Promise?

He paid his Faith Promise.

A few days later he and another fellow went fishing on Lake Erie. When time came to leave, they tried to raise the anchor, but it had snagged on something. After a great deal of pulling and tugging, huffing and puffing, they discovered a new rope snarled around the anchor—and attached to the rope was an anchor just like the one the man had been looking at. He had his new anchor.

He received the Holy Ghost within the month.

A pastor had difficulty with letting down "nets" when the Lord urged him to give $10,000 in the Foreign Missions offering at a general conference.

The pastor argued with God. He had faith to promise $1,000—a single net full—so that's what he gave.

Later a businessman in his church said, "I would have given up to $10,000 in that offering for the church."

The pastor rued letting down only one net.

In another general conference, an appeal went forth for support for overseas literature. The Lord whispered to a missionary seated on the platform.

"Pledge a thousand dollars," came the soft whisper.

The missionary argued with God. He felt that he could afford to pledge for only one net's worth of $100.

The Lord continued to impress him as to what he should commit. Finally the missionary strolled to the microphone, called out the name of his country—and committed $100 for overseas literature.

After the service he walked to the edge of the platform. At the bottom of the steps stood a lady waiting for him to come down. When he reached the floor, the lady told him something that made his heart sink.

"Brother," she said, "my husband said to tell you that he would pay whatever you promised."

The husband was a multimillionaire.

The missionary felt like dropping to his knees and repenting then and there because he had not obeyed the Lord.

Obeying the prompting of the Holy Ghost even to let down a net at all was difficult—at first—for a young Illinois couple with three small children. Especially when the husband was in the construction business. Especially in the middle of a cold, snowy winter in southern Illinois when the man was out of work. Especially when there was no work to be had. Especially since they hadn't the slightest clue how they were going to pay their bills. Especially when they had a house payment due.

Wednesday night: Foreign Missions service. The pastor asked each member of the congregation to kneel and pray and ask the Lord what they should give.

The Lord spoke to the wife and said, "Give five hundred dollars."

"Lord, You know I have no job. I'm staying home to raise our three little ones. Did I hear You right?"

The Lord spoke again, "Five hundred dollars."

As they stood up after praying, her husband asked, "Honey, how much do you think we should give?"

"Five," she whispered.

"Five dollars?"

"No. Five."

He said, "What, fifty dollars?"

"No," she murmured. "The Lord said five hundred dollars."

The husband's jaw dropped. He was speechless. He could say neither yea nor nay. He knew his wife, knew she was aware they had nothing at all in the checking account.

But he wrote the check, praying that they could somehow deposit enough money into the bank so the check wouldn't bounce.

As soon as the service was over, one of the brethren walked up to the husband.

"You have a phone call in the sound room," he said.

The call came from a contractor who had phoned the church, wanting the husband to do some work.

When her husband told his wife what had happened, she could only shake her head in wonder.

The husband's jaw dropped.
He was speechless.

"Can you believe that?" she later asked Jack. "Brother Leaman, no one has ever called my husband at church instead of phoning us at home wanting us to do a job for him."

We were standing there talking when the same brother returned and said, "You have another call."

Talk about the Lord's ways being above our ways! A second contractor called with a construction job for them. Can you imagine calling the church looking for them instead of ringing them at home? How did the contractors even know where to call? This captivating story didn't stop that night, though.

The next morning when the husband left the house, but before he reached the garage, the phone rang. A third contractor called with a job for them! Three different contractors phoned, each offering work for the couple. They got all three jobs. They both recognized the boatful of pressed-down blessings as coming from the hand of the Lord Jesus Christ.

Not all blessings are immediately evident, though. One **Wisconsin** man lost his job after he and his wife made a Faith Promise. In spite of this, they met all their bills, including their Faith Promise.

"We never would have known what it was to trust God if it hadn't been for Faith Promise," the wife said.

The next year when it was time to renew their Faith Promise, the husband told his wife that he had two figures in mind.

"Remember how faithful God has been this past year," she said. "Give the bigger amount because the devil wants you to give the smaller one."

He obeyed his wife, and God continued to bless them both.

An elderly father in **Ohio** left a legacy of giving liberally to missions. After his father's death, the son increased his own giving to equal that of his father's: $1,200 a month. A few weeks after the son committed himself to this amount, a banker friend invited him out to lunch.

"I am going to give you 150 shares in our bank. They are worth $11,000 at the present time," the banker said, smiling at his friend's slack-jawed expression.

The Lord caused this to happen, the man thought. He had no retirement for his family because he had opted out of Social Security years earlier and felt this was God looking out for the family's future.

"God, You always bless the other person," Gina said to herself when during a midweek service she heard another sister testify of the blessings of getting a raise that was twice her year's Faith Promise. However, just

---

God, You always bless the other person instead of me!

---

two days later Gina received a miracle of her own. She had applied for a job a month before and had been bypassed in favor of someone else. When that happened, she asked the hiring person to call her if the other lady did not work out. Well, the hiring person did call her and offered her the job. The amount of her salary increase was twelve times her sacrificial Faith Promise.

A young **Texan** couple with severe financial struggles took a big step to commit even a small monthly amount to Faith Promise. Shortly thereafter, they received a check for $1,000 from American Express.

"I don't know why we received this check from American Express," the young woman told her husband.

"Call them and find out," the husband suggested.

The wife contacted American Express to question the reason for the check.

"You've made an overpayment, ma'am," the AmEx representative replied. "The check is your refund."

"But that could never be," the sister explained. "We could never, never have overpaid that much. We couldn't afford to."

After several more phone conversations, in which the sister repeated that they never had that much money to overpay a credit card charge, the American Express employee replied, "American Express would not make an error. You must have overpaid without realizing it. Please, simply accept the refund!"

Which, of course, they did, realizing immediately that God had smiled upon their sacrifice for the cause of spreading the gospel.

"You are going to have to give yourself out of that hole."

"Pastor, I'm having terrible financial problems," Roy lamented. "I'm so deeply in debt that I don't know what to do. I don't want to declare bankruptcy, but that seems the only solution to my problems. I thought maybe you could give me some advice."

"I can give you some scriptural advice," the pastor said.

"That's the kind of advice I need," the man replied. "Something from the Word of God. I've got to get out of this financial squeeze. I've dug myself into a deep hole."

"You are going to have to give yourself out of that hole," the pastor said.

"Give? Give? Pastor, I have nothing to give. How can I give money I don't have?"

"As a first choice, I'd say foreign missions," the pastor counseled. "Reaching out to the unsaved touches the heart of God. Solomon wrote in Proverbs three, verse five, about trusting in the LORD with all your heart and leaning not unto your own understanding. In verse six Solomon admonished us to acknowledge the Lord in all our ways, and He shall direct our paths. When we are willing to trust in the Lord for direction even when we can't figure everything out, He opens the windows of heaven and pours on us some of His wonderful surprises."

"Spending seems a strange way to get out of my difficulties! Spending got me into this trouble. But I'll do it!"

Roy committed to Faith Promise. One year later he testified and listed thirteen pressed-down blessings the Lord had helped him with over the past year—including getting out of debt.

The following testimony, edited slightly, is taken with permission from the *Oklahoma Beacon.*

I could see absolutely no way out of the financial bind I was in. Each month I had fallen farther and farther behind in my obligations, and deadlines on a couple of debts had now arrived. I still owed my parents for a car they had helped me to purchase after an accident two years earlier had totaled the Toyota I had been driving for five years. Two large, longstanding personal loans haunted me daily. I had never intended to get into such a predicament, but every time it appeared I would have an extra twenty dollars to apply to an obligation, an unforeseen emergency would occur.

I tried my best not to let anxiety take hold. I called my parents and pleaded, "Please help me pray for a financial miracle!" As usual, they were loving and unselfish, offering once again to come to my financial rescue as best they could. But this was not the answer. I asked a dear sister [in Christ] to help me pray for a financial miracle. . . . So we prayed—my parents, [my friend], and I—for a miracle from God. The situation demanded nothing less.

We had been beseeching the Lord for about a month when Brother Jack Leaman from the Foreign Missions Division of the UPC came to our church for our annual Faith Promise service. During the services we were moved and blessed by the reports and testimonies from mission fields around the world. At the close of his message on Sunday morning, Brother Leaman asked each of us to prayerfully consider during the afternoon what God would have us commit by faith in the evening service. I felt that my terrible financial position prohibited any pledge, but nevertheless I carefully probed my "budget" for a

$10 cushion I had built in somewhere. But there really wasn't one. Still, I mentally persisted. If I cut into our necessities somewhere—gas to groceries—just maybe I could come up with $5 . . . $10 . . . or perhaps $15 each month.

As I sat there, half listening, Brother Leaman said something that caught my attention. If I could become a channel for funds to flow into the work of God, how much would I like for God to channel through me? *What a wonderfully, unique way to be used of God,* I thought. I had not made a conscious decision to pledge as yet, but I became increasingly excited with this new concept as I thought about it throughout the afternoon.

"An amount that would seem rather conservative to some budgets was rather enormous to ours."

During the evening service, the urge to put this concept of Faith Promise to the test became stronger and stronger. An amount that would seem rather conservative to some budgets but that was rather enormous to ours stood out strongly in my mind. It was enough to require a direct provision from God. I suppose my faith was still small, because when I filled out the amount of my monthly Faith Promise, I wrote on the card "Up to $50." I was giving God a way out.

But God doesn't need a way out! He has promised—"Give [first], and it shall be given unto you." I had given Him nothing but a promise that I would give back to Him $50 per month if He would bless me with that much left over after our absolute monthly necessities had been met.

Not once after I turned in my pledge card did I feel the customary heaviness of an additional financial obligation. Why should I? I had not assumed an obligation but had offered myself as a "channel" to God. I felt excitement and expectation for what would surely transpire.

The following week was a particularly difficult one at work. I was extremely discouraged, and though I was trying my very best, I felt that my performance was below expectations. Toward the end of the week, the executive director called to me as I walked past his office. Motioning me into his office, he closed the door and then looked at me for a second. My heart pounded unhappily, and I feared what I was about to hear. Any moment now he would begin to say the words that had been going on in my mind all week long—that I was not meeting the expected performance levels.

"I want to tell you something that will make your weekend," he began. Relief had barely penetrated when he continued, "I am going to give you a raise . . . and you deserve it." *A raise! I deserved it?* Shock numbed me, and I stood dumbly. I scarcely heard a word that followed. I finally gained enough sensibility to thank him and returned to my office.

It was not more than an hour or so later that the director stepped into my office. "This must really be your day! We just got word that the governor has approved an across-the-board increase for all state employees. So you're going to get a double raise."

But [the blessing] didn't stop there. A few weeks later the Lord provided me with a part-time job that required just five or six hours a week. And, to make it even better, my daughter and son would be able to accompany me.

So since allowing God to channel $50 per month through me for the cause of Foreign Missions, God has increased my monthly income by $390 clear. Not only have I become able to help with the worldwide mission of reaching the lost, but God has also provided the financial miracle that I had so desperately needed.

Yes, God really does honor Faith Promise. Thank You, Lord, for Faith Promise. Through it, I have learned a valuable lesson: The first step is to give!

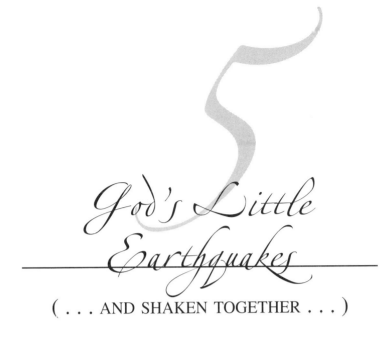

God's Little Earthquakes

(. . . AND SHAKEN TOGETHER . . .)

Jesus, when He walked on earth, was quite the shaker-upper. In fact, He was an upside-downer. More importantly, He was an inside-outer. Here's proof: He shook up the established religious luminaries so badly they wanted to kill Him. He had the audacity to tell them to render unto Caesar what was Caesar's. And He challenged them to look inside the whited sepulchers to see the dry, brittle bones inside them. Jesus was a straight-to-the-heart-of-it sort of guy who was desperately concerned about the heart of a person.

In one of His most famous parables, Jesus revealed four types of people. First was the traveler, an apt representative of the world as a whole. Ambushed by thieves who left him penniless, he lay naked, broken, and bleeding in the dusty Jerusalem-to-Jericho road under an indifferent, merciless sun. Helpless, he was in a condition only to receive.

Second were the thieves. Their nasty me-ness led them to pounce on the hapless wayfarer and strip him of everything he owned and nearly everything of what he was. Their attitude was gimmee-gimmee: *What's yours is mine, and I'm going to take it.*

Third: A priest sauntered along, glimpsed the battered man, and edged away from the fellow. Can't you see him lifting his priestly skirts, not wanting to defile himself with the blood oozing from the inert form? So he scurried away.

Fourth (same type of person): A Levite mimicked the actions of the priest, except he looked at the wounded man a moment longer, perhaps inching closer to examine him before turning away in disgust and hurrying on his way—maybe to revival services! You see, both the priest and the Levite had religious training that, unfortunately, affected the fallen man not one little bit. Their attitude was: *What's mine is mine, and I'm going to keep it.* They were the hoarders.

Then came the good Samaritan. He let his heart be moved with compassion. He cleansed and bandaged the poor fellow's wounds, hoisted him onto his own donkey, and took him to an inn. He stayed at his bedside, tending to his needs all night long. When the Samaritan left the next day, he deposited money for the man's care with the innkeeper and said, "Take care of him; and whatsoever thou spendest more, when I come again, I will repay thee" (Luke 10:35).

Jesus commended the actions of the Samaritan and told His listeners to "Go, and do thou likewise [show mercy]" (Luke 10:37). In other words, have a Samaritan-like attitude toward giving: *What's mine is ours, and I'll share with you.*

In a reversal of the norm, Jesus turned things inside out when He revealed the despised Samaritan to be the good guy, and the revered (at least in their own eyes) priest and Levite as the bad guys. The liberality of the Samaritan contrasted sharply with the stinginess of those who carefully counted out tiny plants and seeds—mint and anise and cumin—to the tenth (was it to make sure God got His ten percent, or were they making sure they

> *Jesus often rattled the cage*
> *of the status quo.*

got their ninety percent?) but ignored the weightier matters of the law: justice, mercy, and faith (Matthew 23:23). What a teeth-gnashing, nail-biting, earth-shaking situation the scribes and Pharisees found themselves in when Jesus exposed their hearts' rotten attitudes!

What greater mercy can we show the beaten, bruised world than to have a Samaritan spirit of giving: I'll give you a share of my Jesus by sending Samaritans (missionaries) to you?

A pastor thought of a unique and clever way to answer a missionary's plea for help. A church being built in Uruguay needed a roof, and the minister wanted his Ohio church to be the church that showed mercy by providing funds for it.

So one Sunday, he asked his congregation, "How many of you would give me one hundred dollars for one thousand?"

Hands shot up into the air.

With a smile, the pastor explained that the one thousand was not dollars but pesos! Then he told the saints about the church in Uruguay that needed a roof.

Most of the hands stayed up, even when the saints realized that their giving one hundred dollars was considerably more money than their receiving one thousand Uruguayan pesos!

The pastor raised the $1,500 needed for the roof.

A Canadian church had a roof, but it leaked even though it had been repaired the previous fall at a cost of $900.

The church had many needs of its own in addition to the pesky problem of the leaky roof; nevertheless, the pastor invited a missionary to present Faith Promise to his congregation. The twenty-one adults in the service committed themselves to $750 a month, even though the money could have paid for more and very necessary repairs on the roof.

One day shortly after the missions' conference, one of the men in the church climbed to the roof to try to determine the cause of the problem. Suddenly a head, then the upper body, of a stranger appeared over the eaves.

"Are you having trouble with the roof?" the stranger inquired.

"We sure are!" the saint exclaimed. "We had this roof repaired just a few months ago, but it still leaks."

"I'm a roofer," the man on the ladder explained. "Once every year I donate a free roof to someone. If you agree not to tell anyone about my offer, I'll put a new roof

114

on this building. It won't cost you a cent."

So the church traded their silence for a new roof valued at $6,000.

Oh, yes. The new roof came with a twenty-five-year written guarantee.

It's easy for the Lord to leap from roofs to parking lots and driveways in response to His people when they unstintingly give. For one example, a Florida church had taken pledges to blacktop their church parking lot. Two weeks later, in the church's annual missions' conference, the pastor rattled his church for a minute when he asked them to cancel their pledges for the parking lot.

"Use the money you pledged for the blacktop in making your Faith Promise," he told his congregation.

The church responded with a great outpouring of funds for Faith Promise. Before the month passed, the pastor was given $30,000 to have the parking lot blacktopped.

In a neighboring state, a businessman told Jack what happened when the congregation built their new church.

"Brother Leaman," the man said, "I agreed to pay for the blacktopping of the driveway. It cost $103,000. But that same month, I received a contract for $4 million! I'd given in the past and learned that God always blesses the giver."

The final coating on blacktop stories, however, comes from a giver's interaction with a missionary. Brother Louis Louw, missionary to Namibia, left his wife and daughter in one state while he traveled on deputation to another state. There the engine in his converted motor home bus conked out, stranding him. The vehicle needed a new engine, but he lacked money to buy one.

Brother Louw phoned his wife, and together they prayed for the money needed for the motor home engine.

When Sister Louw related her husband's difficulty to the local pastor, he took up a special offering for the needed motor and sent it to the missionary.

A few days later, with a new engine in the motor home, Brother Louw picked up his wife and daughter at the church.

A young man who attended the church recognized Brother Louw and introduced himself.

"My wife and I had been saving money to have our driveway blacktopped," he told the missionary. "We had saved $380, but we figured your need was a whole lot greater than having our driveway surfaced, so we gave it all toward the price of your new motor.

"The next week we came home to find our driveway had been blacktopped! We were shaken up because we had not ordered it to be done. Furthermore, we were worried about receiving a bill from the blacktop people, because we couldn't pay it.

"Brother Louw, a few days later the blacktop folks were back, blacktopping a neighbor's driveway. They had mistakenly paved our driveway the week before. We got our driveway surfaced for free!"

Parking lots and driveways are for cars, right? Here's a collection of car-as-God's-shake-together-pay-back-for-faithful-giving stories:

A lady in North Carolina made her Faith Promise while

having problems with her van. Although told that it would cost her $1,000 to have the van repaired, she spent the money on her Faith Promise. She had no more problems with the vehicle, even though it had not been repaired.

After giving $25 a month to Faith Promise, a couple increased their commitment to $50 a month. Then he was laid off from his job.

"Now what are we going to do?" his wife asked him.

"Maybe this will be the making of us," he replied.

Shortly afterwards, the husband's former employer sold his business, and the new owner called the man back to work. He not only received a raise, but the job also provided him a car to drive.

A pastor's wife in **Kentucky** felt she needed to upgrade her car. Instead of buying a new car, however, she and her husband decided to get another used car and apply the difference in payments between a new and used car to increase their Faith Promise. A couple in their church, hearing about their plan, handed them a check for $10,000 and instructed them to apply it toward the purchase of a new car.

An **Indiana** man had to borrow $60 to pay his Faith Promise. The family's finances were so straitened that their car had been repossessed. So when a wealthy, elderly lady requested the man's wife to pick her up at the airport, the wife had to borrow a car.

"Where is your car?" the elderly lady asked.

Reluctantly, the woman admitted that it had been repossessed.

"Let's go look at cars," the wealthy woman suggested.

"Oh, no," the woman replied. "We can't do that. We have no money to buy a car."

"Let's look anyway," she insisted.

So the two women drove to a car lot and began to look at used cars. Before long, the elderly lady wanted to go inside the sales building.

"Let's look at the new cars," she said.

Within a few minutes, the wealthy woman wrote a check for a new Century Buick and gave the keys to the car to the astonished and very grateful woman!

After two years of giving, a couple had increased their Faith Promise from $50 to $75 a month. Within a few weeks, they learned they'd won a seven-day Caribbean cruise to the Virgin Islands, all expenses paid. At $3,000, the cruise was valued at more than three times their year's missions commitment.

A year later, the couple increased their Faith Promise to $100 a month, and a year after that, to $150 a month. What a shaking they received when the husband was told he'd won a Buick LeSabre right off the assembly line at work! Over five thousand names from his shop had been entered in the drawing to receive this five millionth Buick, worth over $25,000. And the car was tax-free.

A lady had already been blessed after meeting her Faith Promise, but the Lord had an even greater blessing in store for her. An uncle told her he had a car for her.

"Uncle, I thank you," she replied, "but I can't afford any higher car payment than I already have."

"No," he insisted, "I want you to come. I'll give you three cars to choose from."

So the woman drove to see her uncle and look at the cars he'd set aside for her to consider. The choice was easy: She wanted a white car, and one of the cars was white.

"It's yours," the uncle said. "It's free."

The car was valued at $17,000.

From roofs to driveways to cars to basements, the Lord sends shockwaves of blessings to those who deny themselves to put Him first.

For a reason only God knew, a Canadian man came to a Friday night missionary service with $700 in his pocket. He had been saving money for a much needed central heating unit for his home.

"Put the $700 in the offering," the Lord whispered to him.

I can't, Lord, the man thought. *You know I've been saving and saving for a central heating unit. That $700 will make a good down payment on it.*

"Yes, I know," the Lord seemed to say. "But you just called me Lord. How can I be Lord if you don't listen to me?"

The man slipped the money into an envelope and dropped it into the offering. A great sense of rightness and peace washed over him, and when he crawled into bed that night, he didn't roll and toss, worrying about what he'd done.

When he opened the back door the next morning, a large box blocked his way. His breath caught in his throat as he read the lettering on the box. The brand-new furnace inside was worth far more than the $700 he'd put in the offering the night before.

To this day, he doesn't know who put the furnace on his back porch.

A **Kentucky** man forked over $600 for repairs on his furnace a week before the annual missions' conference at his church. When the time came for him to make his Faith Promise commitment, he jotted down $100 a month.

The next day, the newly repaired heat pump rattled and banged. Realizing the costliness of the ensuing repair bill, he bowed his head.

"Lord," he prayed, "You know I can't afford the expense of another repair bill right now. You'll just have to pay the bill." Laying aside his worries, he called the heating company and arranged for a serviceman to meet him at the house later that day.

After working almost three hours, the repairman entered the house with the bill. He reviewed the invoice with the homeowner and revealed that the heat pump had a Freon leak and a copper line that needed to be replaced. The total bill was in excess of $460.

But the serviceman had written "No charge" across the bottom of the statement.

"The work isn't directly related to last week's problem," the man explained. "But this problem should have been caught last week when the first repairs were made, so I wrote this up as a 'callback.'"

The homeowner could hardly wait for the repairman to leave so he could praise God for what He'd done. Then he called his pastor, so the pastor could rejoice with him.

From roof to driveway to cars to basements to a house . . . that was stalled in being built because, although they had run out of money in building their new home, a couple felt impressed to make a $30 a week Faith Promise commitment. Before the month passed, the man's father gave them $10,000 to use in finishing the house.

. . . and what's inside it—oh, can't you hear the Lord chuckle as we peek inside the structure?

There sit two nice loveseats, purchased at one-third their normal cost, obtained by a young couple who had increased their Faith Promise by one whole week's pay!

A glance into the kitchen reveals a stove, dishwasher, microwave oven, and a refrigerator, given after a husband and wife with several financial needs made a Faith Promise of $400 a month.

Furniture filled a Bible school student's house, too. He couldn't decide whether to give $10 or $20 as his commitment, but when Jack emphasized the "faith" part of giving, the young man opted for the greater amount.

"Since then," he wrote Jack, "God has supplied for every commitment. Within three months I was able to purchase a brand-new washer and dryer in cash. Some other saints gave us a hide-a-bed, and others gave us dressers.

"More than any material need, God has increased my faith that if we will give to Him, then He will move on men to give to us. Praise the Lord! He is confirming His Word with signs following."

Walk—no, tiptoe—down the hall, for in a lovely nursery lies a newborn. He really is a miracle baby. His mom and dad had been discussing the possibility of starting a family, but the doctor had said that her chance of conceiving a child was slim until her health problem could be resolved.

Then the date for their church's annual missions' service arrived. The pair had decided what to commit to Faith Promise, but when the time came to ink in that amount, God seemed to say, "Double what you planned to give."

So she did, feeling assured that if she stepped out in faith, God would give her the desire of her heart. Within months she was expecting a baby. All her health problems cleared up, and the couple's first child was born one year to the day of the Faith Promise service.

One year after that, the proud father came to Brother Leaman after their Saturday night missions' service. He was holding the year-old baby boy.

"Brother Leaman," he said, "this is our Faith Promise baby."

No house would be complete without storage places such as cupboards . . . A lady made a Faith Promise of $100 although she didn't have it. The same month she went to the grocery store and dropped her name in a box like all the other customers did. Her name was drawn, and she won $5,000 worth of groceries. Her "empty basket" filled her cupboard shelves!

. . . and closets—with purses and wallets in them.

The day after she and her husband had made a Faith Promise of $50 a month even with a stretched-thin budget, the wife found fifty dollars in her purse.

"Look what I found," she exulted, waving the money in front of her husband. "Now I can go shopping."

"Don't you dare," the husband retorted. "That's our Faith Promise money. That fifty dollars is from God, and we don't want to spend God's money."

Put that way, the wife agreed.

Some additional testimonies of purses unexpectedly padded after their owners made Faith Promise commitments include the following:

The tale of the wayward pen: Before she knew it, a lady contemplating a Faith Promise of $10 a month added a zero, making her contribution $100 a month instead.

"I was shocked when I realized what I had done," she reported.

A few months later she had another report; not only had she been able to pay the $100 each month, but she had received around $1,300 she had not expected.

The tale of a bust gone boom: A man's flourishing business had flattened like a fried egg after the 9/11 tragedy. In the spring of the following year, he felt God nudging him to make a Faith Promise commitment. He argued with the Lord, reminding God that his business had gone bust. Finally, he obeyed the Spirit's urging and committed himself to a monthly missions offering. Two weeks later, he was startled when orders started pouring in. He then realized that the Lord was honoring his step of faith.

The narrative about an unsaved spouse: A wheelchair-bound husband upset his unsaved wife when he made a Faith Promise commitment without checking with her about it.

"We've always talked financial things over," she reminded him.

"I'm sorry," he admitted. "You're right. I should have discussed it with you first."

The husband felt bad about not including his wife in his Faith Promise decision and asked the Lord for help. A few days later his hospital called and told him that one of his bills had been reduced by $150. He was elated, because after his $120 for the year Faith Promise had been paid, they'd be $30 ahead. His amazed wife listened as the young man explained that he felt the $150 reduction was an answer from the Lord.

The story of the out-of-the-blue check: Within two months of making a $25 Faith Promise, a man had received pay raises of more than two dollars an hour. He had already received back more than three times his Faith Promise.

Then the phone rang.

After a brief conversation, the man dropped the phone back into its cradle. He turned to his wife with a stunned look on his face.

"Is something wrong?" she asked, alarmed by his expression. "Who was that on the phone?"

"The personnel department from my old job," he replied. "They're sending me a check."

"A check?" she queried. "What for? How much?"

"Profit sharing," he replied. "I'd forgotten all about it. It's for twelve hundred dollars."

The case of the wooden nickel: A lady from a nursing home attended a Sunday morning missionary service. She wanted to give but had very little money. She had a wooden nickel and put it in the offering hoping they could get something out of it for the missionary. That night in the service the pastor held up the wooden nickel and told the congregation her story to see if he could get any money out of it for the missionary. People started pledging $10, $25, $50, $100 and more for the nickel. Before it was over, $1,250 had been given for the cause of reaching the lost. (This story appeared in many newspapers around the world, including the military *Stars and Stripes*.)

Can you imagine this precious lady's joy when she learned the ultimate value of her wooden nickel? What a filling of the basket she had emptied by faith!

The collection of a class-action check: In 1970, a man took out a life insurance policy on himself.

"The policy will be paid up in ten years," the insurance agent assured him.

However, that did not prove to be the case. Finally, a group of disgusted and disgruntled policyholders brought a class-action suit against the company. The policyholders won their case.

On December 29, 2000, the man received his portion of the settlement.

"Brother Leaman, at the October missions' conference in our church, my wife and I doubled our commitment and we began supporting Home Missions, too," he told Jack. "The check I received covered both our Faith Promise and our Home Missions commitment for the year—with money left over! Although I have been in the church for over forty years, this has been one of the greatest faith builders that has ever happened to us."

What are closets without clothes? These two closets were filled as a result of Faith Promises:

"Mama, can I empty my bank and give the money to the missionaries?" asked a little five-year-old boy after listening attentively to the missionary in a missions' service in his church.

His mom and dad sat down with him.

"Are you sure this is what you want to do?" they asked.

"Yes," the child said without hesitation.

So his parents allowed him to make the desired offering.

This happened just before Easter. A lady in the church, knowing the family had little money, approached the boy's mother.

"What are you doing for Easter clothes for your three boys?" she asked. "I have some clothes at home. Would you care if I brought them and gave them to your family?"

The mother consented, and the lady brought the clothes for the family.

When the mother unfolded the clothes, she found five new suits and three sport jackets with matching outfits—and all of them fit the five-year-old!

For two years, a teenage girl had been giving to Faith Promise. When time came for her third commitment to missions, her father felt she shouldn't increase her giving. But when commitment time rolled around, she increased her giving by 33 percent over the previous year. After church, she told her dad what she had done.

Within the month she received a box in the mail from a friend in Florida. Opening the box, she pulled out three lovely, new dresses. The dresses were valued at over $500.

The rest of the family was shocked.

And what would a house be without children to make it a home? Even kids can get into the giving act!

Our missionary to **Uruguay** taught the nationals that they should start saving one peso per day to help reach the lost. A woman spread the teaching into the interior of the country and then returned home. A month later she returned to the interior and was amused when a little girl asked if she could give.

"Of course you may," the woman answered, expecting a peso or two from the child.

The child handed thirty pesos to the lady.

"My dad gave me a peso every day for candy," the little girl explained, "but I saved them all. It makes me feel good to give."

In **Ohio**, a six-year-old girl made her Faith Promise of $1 a month. During the conference, a special missionary offering was taken, and she gave her whole month's allowance of $4. Soon after, someone gave her $5. The little girl was excited about what the Lord had done for her.

A ten-year-old **Kentucky** boy gave all of his monthly $5 allowance for his Faith Promise commitment. His grandfather started giving him $5 a month shortly afterwards. So what did the child do? The next year he joyfully doubled his Faith Promise!

In **Illinois,** a twelve-year-old boy made a $4 a month Faith Promise. That month, he received a $48 check from an insurance company as a settlement for an accident he had been in with his mother months earlier. He had no idea that the check would be coming, and neither did the mother!

A sixteen-year-old **Ohio** girl gave this testimony:

> I'm sixteen years old, and last year I committed $20 a month for my Faith Promise. Over the course of this year, I received two raises at my job and I was picked for employee of the month twice. I've also been blessed at my school as I was inducted into the National Honor Society and I was selected as a delegate to the Teen Leadership Conference sponsored by my school district. In my toughest year of high school my grades are the best they've ever been.

A seventeen-year-old boy in **Alaska** made a Faith Promise of $20 a month. Soon after that service he received an unexpected check. Also he was promoted on his job over six others who were ahead of him.

On a nice summer evening in **Indiana**, a pastor taught the meaning of Partners in Missions to the church leaders and Sunday school staff. A little nine-year-old girl listened very carefully.

At the end of the session, the child excitedly tugged on her mom's hand. "Mom, will he [the pastor] take a kid's money?" She had felt the Lord talking to her to give to missions.

The mother immediately took her daughter out to the hall where she could see the world map and all the pictures of the UPCI missionaries.

"Mom, I want my own missionary to support, and I know who it is."

"Honey, where will you get the money?" her mom asked.

"My allowance is five dollars a month," she replied. "I want to give that."

"If you give your entire allowance to missions, you'll have nothing left to spend the rest of the month. You couldn't go to the mall, either."

"Oh, yes, I will," the little girl promptly answered, "because the missionary said if we give to missions, Jesus would see that we also would have what we need." She looked at all the pictures and then pointed to the picture of Brother Robert McFarland and Sister Beth McFarland (Israel/Palestine) and said, "That's the one I want to send my allowance to."

"Why did you choose them?" the mother asked.

The child replied, "He smiled a lot when he visited our church, and he lives [in the country] where Jesus lived."

"I don't know how my daughter manages, but as soon as she's given her allowance, she immediately makes out her missions envelope," her mother reported. "Yet she always has money in her purse. Folks ask her to run errands or do them favors, and their 'tips' supply her with spending money and, most of all, prove God's faithfulness."

In a missions' service in May 2006, **Brother Terry Black** of Memphis, Tennessee, strongly endorsed the Faith Promise program. His testimonial, edited for print, illustrates the shaken-together blessing afforded a Samaritan-like giving church.

> It's my charge before God to lead this church into paths and pastures that are healthy, godly forums. The only thing that I believe that we should understand is that when the Spirit speaks, we should be willing to respond to what the Lord is dealing with us about. We should be sacrificial in our giving. We should be faithful. I am absolutely convinced that, over the years, the commitments that have been made by this church have brought the blessing of God in many ways, including financial blessing.
>
> Seventeen years ago when we bought this property, we took the step by faith. We doubled our note—we were paying the note on the old property; we were paying the note on this property. When we bought this property, the old property was appraised at a disappointing $300,000. We owed over $200,000 on that property. We were paying $5,000 a month on our note. When

we bought this property, it was another $5,000 a month that we had to pay.

When we bought this property, we had a house and fifteen acres of land that we weren't going to be using until the airport bought us. We decided to rent because we really didn't know when the airport was going to buy our property.

We decided to rent the house for $3,000 a month. That would have been 60 percent of our note. The first man who called rented it until the airport bought the property. Within thirty or sixty days after the renter decided to move out, the airport came through with an offer and bought our building.

When we bought this property, we bought it on a floating interest. Interest rates at that time were extremely high. Every single month we owned that property from the time we bought it until the airport bought us out, the interest went down. I'm convinced that the federal government was blessed and the whole nation was blessed because we decided to step out and support missions and expand the kingdom in this city! Between the rent and the interest rate going down, the Lord made it all affordable for us. And then the airport came through and bought the old property.

The old property was appraised at $300,000. We were disappointed. They compared our property to old garages and old auto body shops.

When we got that appraisal, I thought, *Dear Lord, if we don't get more than $300,000 for this property, we're going to be sunk. We can't make the move.* Long story short, the appraisal came through from the airport for $1.1 million, and that's what they paid.

We went through the whole process of designing and building this building, and folks, if you know anything at all about building, you'll know that what I'm about to tell you is just about an absolute impossibility. Elder Brother Kelly is here and he can attest to what I'm about to say—33,000 square feet we built right here. We paid $1.49 million for this property, which is a little over fifty dollars a square foot turnkey to build this building.

Some of you were here when we'd just moved into the building in November. On a Monday morning in January with record low temperatures, the boiler went down, the sprinkler system froze. Brother Trimble called me, and he said, "Brother Black, you're not going to believe this, but I'm standing here in the building, and there's a foot of water in the sanctuary and you could ride a raft right down the center hall."

I got over here and water was pouring out of the vestibule. Some of you even came by that day and stood in the sanctuary and wept because the enemy had attacked our brand-new building. But how many times have I said here not to determine too quickly what is a curse and what is a blessing?

Many times it is difficult to know the difference when you're in the middle of a situation. The insurance company came through and assigned a $363,000 figure to the damage.

I asked the adjuster point-blank, "Do we have to spend that much money?"

He said, "You can spend it or you can do whatever you want to with the check. You can build it back or whatever, but that's the check you're getting."

I said, "Thank you very much."

We restored all of this for about $50,000 and put $310,000 in the bank.

Three years later, right after a record missions—I should make this point: all this time and during every year, we're giving to missions, and every year, missions giving is increasing and God is blessing in financial ways and also the church is growing—I drove around here one morning and looked upon the building as I do every morning when I come through here, admiring what the Lord has given us, thanking Him for it—and the steeple was gone.

I thought, *Somebody has stolen our steeple. Why would somebody want our steeple and how would they get it off our building?* I drove into the parking lot and saw the steeple laying over in the grass, the windows were busted out on the front here, and the panels were pulled up. We had to go through the whole [rebuilding] thing again. We called the insurance company, and they sent their crews out and assigned a $330,000 or $340,000 figure to the damage. It was all their doing.

They decided to give us $250,000 for the roof.

I said, "What do I have to do with this check? Do I have to spend it on builders? Do I have to spend it on construction?"

They said, "You can spend it however you want to spend it, but that's the value we assigned to your damage."

I said, "Thank you very much."

I called Brother Mark and asked if he would come look at the roof, telling him they wanted us to spend $250,000 to fix it. Brother Mark went and bought about twelve dollars worth of screws and fixed our $250,000 repair job, and with about $30,000 replaced the steeple and repaired all the damage. The Lord put another $300,000 in the bank, and that $600,000 is over on Bill Morris Parkway right now getting ready for what the Lord is fixing to do in the future.

I'm telling The Pentecostal Church today that when you support the kingdom of God, He will support you! Hallelujah! That's what it's all about: Give to the Lord! So I'm standing here telling you that I've already been to that precipice years ago, and I debated all night long on Saturday night before missions' conference, saying, "Lord, I need to do something. I need to say something to the people because we've got a building program that we've got to be a part of. I don't want to shortchange the building program, so I need these people to give everything they've got to missions, and there won't be anything left over for the building."

I'm telling you the Holy Ghost spoke to me sixteen years ago on that Saturday night and

"Son, you worry about My kingdom, and I'll worry about your building."

said, "Son, you worry about My kingdom, and I'll worry about your building." And not one day since then have I second-guessed that. Every year we've come here and done exactly what we're doing today, and you folks sacrifice and give. And every year the Lord keeps blessing The Pentecostal Church with souls and keeps blessing us with property. I am telling you that so far net receiving that we have received more financially than we have given in as a church. So the bottom line is that if we had to choose, I'm telling you now, that if we had to choose between a building or missions, I would put the building on the back burner and I would tell this church, encourage you to give to missions even if it means we don't have a hope of building a building, because I know that when people get behind the will of God, and they support what is valuable to the heart and the mind of God, He will make sure that what we are concerned about and what we desire will come to pass.

Good-Samaritan-type giving can shake the earth. Then God will give shaken-together blessings.

Scoop and Shovel, Anyone?

(. . . AND RUNNING OVER . . .)

Faith has feet. And legs. Arms. And hands.

James, the brother of Jesus, wrote it this way: "I will shew thee my faith by my works. . . . Faith without works is dead" (James 2:18, 20).

Faith is always up and doing, working, operating, producing. If faith isn't functioning, it's dead.

A Philippine pastor's faith was very much alive one day. His wife was hungry, his own stomach was growling, and his several children were (as kids say) st-ar-ar-ar-ving.

They had no food. None.

So he put feet on his faith and went to prayer. In a short while, he arose from his knees, roused his wife, and proved that his faith was alive and well.

"Put some water on the stove to heat for rice," he instructed his wife.

"Husband, we have no rice."

"Please, do as I say," he insisted.

Obediently, she placed a pan of water on the stove. But looking at the empty cupboard, she was thinking, *Has my husband lost his mind?*

Then the pastor turned to his children.

"Kids, set the table."

They did so, wondering about their dad's mental aberrations.

"Let's sit down," he said.

Chairs scraped the floor; the water bubbled cheerily on the stove. The only other sound was that of the pastor's voice as he asked a blessing on the empty plates and bare table.

Then—a knock at the door!

When he opened the door, the pastor nearly tumbled over a 100-pound bag of groceries, which included a 50-pound sack of rice! As he wrestled the food into the house, he saw his family with hands raised, praising the Lord for the miracle they had just witnessed.

Dinner preparation went quickly that night. After all, the water for the rice already bubbled in the pan!

In making a Faith Promise commitment, the individual puts feet on his faith. He or she steps out in faith, believing that God will supply the funds that will enable him or her to pay God what was promised.

The following testimonies have been gathered from all parts of the country, from saints, pastors, and missionaries. The main thing they have in common is that when God supplied the need, He poured so much into their empty baskets, the baskets overflowed.

"Lord, that's an impossible amount," a young woman

in **Tennessee** whispered. "There is just no way I can promise that much."

The irresistible prompting of the Spirit, however, caused her to write that "impossible" figure on her Faith Promise card anyway.

Then the Lord showed her some sacrifices she could make to meet her goal.

Two months after she made her commitment, she had her work reviewed—and found a 15.9 percent raise on her paycheck.

The Lord showed her some sacrifices she could make to meet her goal.

A month later, she started construction on a new home. Upon closing on the house, she was amazed that the closing cost was only $277 when she'd expected to pay between $1,000 and $1,200! Furthermore, the interest on the mortgage was only 5.9 percent.

Then, to add to the overflow, she was able to get a new car with low interest and low payments.

She summed her experiences up by saying, "You can never outgive God."

An **Ohio** man who works in a bank had applied for a different position earlier and had been passed over. Three days after making his first Faith Promise, he was given the job he wanted. The new position meant a 40 percent increase over his previous salary. He felt rewarded for obeying the leading of the Spirit in making his commitment.

A **Michigan** couple testified that five years earlier they committed $25 a month to Faith Promise. The wife's income included a salary plus commission, which usually ran between $2,000 and $3,000 a year. As they continued to give, her commission mushroomed to an astonishing $13,000. They now give $300 a month. As God blessed them, they have increased their giving.

An **Ohio** man made his first Faith Promise for $100 a month.

The next year he doubled it to $200 a month.

That year his income swelled to $80,000.

The next year he doubled his commitment to $400 a month.

That year he went in business for himself and his income doubled to $160,000.

Minnesota: Shortly after the church's missions' service in which the pastor asked his congregation to double their previous year's Faith Promise, a young man stood and testified that he had tripled his past year's commitment.

"I just received a raise of $6 an hour," he reported.

That brought his pay to nearly $24 an hour, which, at that time, was excellent pay for a nineteen-year-old with only a high school diploma.

A disabled **North Carolina** woman had been denied a pension several times. The family, however, made an $80 a month Faith Promise commitment. A short time afterward, she was notified that her pension had been approved for $484 a month.

That more than took care of their Faith Promise. The overflow called for a figurative scoop: the pension was retroactive for five years, which meant a bonus of over $29,000!

Illinois: "Brother Leaman, I was going to put down five dollars a month," a man told Jack. "I had been in the hospital but I had no medical insurance, so I was worrying about paying off that hospital bill. When I filled out my card, though, I wrote one hundred dollars. A week later I received a notice from the hospital that my $1,500 in hospital charges had been remitted."

The "legs" a Michigan woman put on her faith was a postage stamp!

The "legs" a **Michigan** woman put on her faith was a United States postage stamp! Her husband had been injured on his job. Three surgeries provided no remedy, and he had been unable to work for four years.

Seven months after his injury he hired a lawyer and filed for disability.

"Maybe I need to write a letter to the judge," the wife suggested to their lawyer.

"There's no need of that," the lawyer replied.

After four denials, however, the lawyer said there was nothing else he could do but reapply and start all over again.

"I still believe God has given me words to write the judge," the wife declared. Finally she wrote the letter and sent it to the judge.

About that time, in a Faith Promise service, the Lord gave them direction as to the amount of their commitment even though the past year had been very difficult with house payment, car payment, insurance, utilities, and all the other normal household expenses. Only a miracle enabled them to keep their bills current.

They stepped out in faith and committed $75 a month for missions. Two days after the service, they received a check for nearly $20,000 for back pay on disability. They also learned they would start receiving an income to meet their monthly bills.

When we do what we can do, God does what we can't.

Louisiana: "Lord, if You will give me the money, I'll send a thousand dollars to Madagascar to help build a church there," a man promised the Lord.

About a week later, the government discovered an error in paying his wife's disability and put several thousand dollars into their account.

A **Michigan** pastor took Larry, a man in his church, with him to hold a Faith Promise service. Larry made a $100 per month Faith Promise.

A few days later the local pastor called his friend.

"I'll send you Larry's monthly commitment," he said.

"No, Larry believes in giving and that the Lord will bless him," the visiting pastor replied.

Two weeks later Larry called his pastor. His excitement hummed through the phone wires.

"Pastor, I've just been given a thousand dollars from a man to whom I loaned money seven years ago! I never expected to get it back."

A **Mississippi** businessman was about to bid on a job when he followed the leading of the Lord and committed

$12,000 to foreign missions. A bit fearful of the yo-yo inflation at that time, he wondered what kind of profit he'd net on the job.

A bit fearful of the yo-yo inflation at that time, a businessman wondered what kind of profit he'd net on the job.

It turns out he needn't have wondered. The same week, a man walked into his office and placed a check for $10,000 on his desk.

"I've owed this to you for years," the fellow said. "I figured it was time I paid it back."

A missionary on deputation, while attending a district men's retreat, felt impressed to give a home missionary pastor an offering.

The next morning before the service, he slipped the home missionary $250.

Lord, You know I really needed this myself, he thought. *But I want to obey You, and You prompted me to give this offering.*

Later in the day session of the conference, the speaker called the foreign missionary to the front.

"Stand right here, Brother," the speaker said to the astonished missionary. Then he challenged the congregation to give the missionary an offering.

The ministers poured out of their pews, pulling out their wallets as they did so. Some put money in his hands, while others stuffed bills into his pockets.

"Somebody get a wastebasket," the speaker said.

The missionary stared in awe as the wastebasket filled. The offering totaled over $3,300.

Colorado: A woman expected to receive a small inheritance of $2,400 from a deceased uncle.

"I'll just give the whole $2,400 as my Faith Promise," she said to herself as she inserted $200 in the appropriate space on the Faith Promise card.

Within the month she received her inheritance.

The amount of her inheritance didn't come near what she had expected.

It was ten times that amount: she received $24,000.

Kentucky: "Lord, I'm really stepping out on faith in this one," a man murmured to himself as he filled out his Faith Promise card. "I don't have the money but You're talking to me about this, so here goes."

With that, he penciled in the amount he felt the Lord wanted him to give: $300 a month.

Within the month he got a new job paying three times what his old salary paid. Then severance pay from his old job spilled out of the basket. It was enough to pay his year's Faith Promise.

A **Texas** businessman made a monthly Faith Promise of $2,000 before the Sunday night service. After the service he added $500, making his monthly offering a total of $2,500.

He later stated that within the month God showed him how he could reduce the cost of operating his business by $2,500 a month.

Another man from that same **Texas** church received

twenty times his yearly Faith Promise in just one business transaction!

I should commit $500 a month to foreign missions, a **Florida** man thought to himself. *But that is a lot of money and more than I can really afford to give. My wife and I are in the process of adopting two children, and that's going to cost us twenty thousand dollars.* So during the service he promised $100 a month.

He stared at the bill in disbelief. Surely there should be more zeros!

After the commitments were totaled, the pastor said, "Folks, we've fallen short by four hundred dollars on what our church should have committed."

Shock rippled through the man who had promised $100 instead of the $500 the Lord had impressed on him, and he decided to make up the difference after all.

He faithfully met his commitment all during the adoption process. Then he received the bill from his lawyer.

He stared at the bill in disbelief. Surely he wasn't reading it right! Shouldn't there be another zero, and shouldn't that be a comma instead of a period?

The lawyer charged the couple $26.00 instead of the $20,000 plus they'd expected to pay.

This is the scoop and shovel part: A few months later he received a raise that upped his income by more than $62,000 a year!

A **Minnesota** man made a Faith Promise of $100 a month.

When the pastor saw the commitment he shook his head. "It will take a real miracle for that man to be able to keep that commitment," he told Jack. "I know his income, so he has truly stepped out in faith."

The miracle happened!

Within a few days that man's supervisor called him into the office.

"Joe," the supervisor said. "I have good news for you. We overlooked a raise you should have had months ago."

The raise was enough to pay his entire year's commitment!

"Pastor, I'm going to pay my Faith Promise one month at a time," Joe said.

He paid only the first month's Promise and reneged on the rest.

From that time on his finances went downhill. The figurative shovel, instead of scooping up blessings, dug a hole.

For five months, an **Ohio** pastor had tried to sell his home but had not received a single offer. During their missions' conference, he renewed his financial commitment as he felt the Lord lead. Five days after he made his Faith Promise, he sold his home for the asking price—and the buyer paid cash for the home!

A contractor in **Indiana** felt impressed to give a 1957 Chevrolet to a National in Israel. The popular antique would sell for between twenty-five and thirty thousand dollars here. Within seven weeks, in a dead housing market, the contractor had contracts to build seven new homes.

Miles farther south in **Kentucky**, an older couple had an amount in mind for their Faith Promise commitment, but God impressed the husband that it should be five times that amount. They changed their minds and made the commitment God impressed upon them.

The husband, a contractor, had had a house for sale for nine months. The interest on the building loan was gobbling up any profit he anticipated.

"Just bring me an offer," he had told the real estate agent.

After his commitment, he received a call from the agent.

"I have a contract on that house. It's for your asking price," the agent told the relieved and thankful contractor.

The contractor turned around and built another home for a couple who wanted a house like the one he'd just sold.

"God gave me two sales as a result of our obeying the Lord that night," he reported to Leaman.

Brother Drury, at that time director of the Tupelo Children's Mansion in Tupelo, **Mississippi**, attended a missionary service during a time when the Mansion's own needs pressed urgently upon him. Brother Drury felt God speak to him to give $500 for an overseas missions project that was presented. Later he committed $100 more, and then, before the service ended, he promised another $100.

Earlier that day he had laid the Mansion's needs before the Lord. Within a few days enough money arrived at the Mansion to pay for the needs and left a surplus of $2,200.

Not only that, the figurative feet that Brother Drury put on his faith that night walked on new carpet that was soon donated to the Mansion.

At a **general conference**, a missionary was called to the platform. He had been traveling Eastern Europe, endeavoring to keep the works functioning smoothly, and in doing so had run up a deficit in excess of $60,000.

"I'd like to have 120 pastors come to the platform and shake the missionary's hand and tell him they would send $500 to erase the deficit account," the emcee announced.

A pastor sitting in the bleachers wanted to contribute but knew the church had no money in its missions account. In addition, the church folks were fixing up a missions room in their church building so the missionaries would have a pleasant place to stay when visiting their church.

At the podium, the emcee was calling out the number of pastors who were responding to his invitation.

"Brother Leaman, when I heard the number eighty-five called out, I could not sit in my seat any longer," he later told Jack. "I got up and walked down the steps and marched onto the platform. When I reached the missionary, I shook his hand and told him I'd send him five hundred dollars next week.

"I don't know why I said 'next week,' because we didn't have it. But I had said it. Before I reached my seat, I passed a man from my church who knew we didn't have it. I patted him on the shoulder and said, 'God will provide.'"

Two days later, while the pastor was in his home church, a man strode into the building and handed the pastor a check for $8,500.

"This is for your church," the man said.

The money enabled the church to finish the missionary room, pay the $500 to the missionary, and tuck some away in the bank.

In **Maryland**, the pastor's twenty-one-year-old son made a Faith Promise of $150 a month, or $1,800 for the year. Not long after the service, he got a new job with a pay increase over his old job of $18,000 a year. What a blessing to scoop up!

A young man walked into church in **Pennsylvania** on Faith Promise night. He felt quite satisfied, for he intended to double his previous year's commitment.

But as he strode to his seat, the Lord spoke to him and said, "Double that amount."

He obeyed, and shortly thereafter he received a 400 percent raise.

Wisconsin: An overseer who had ten men working under him also had a small business. In July the man made his Faith Promise commitment for $250 a month.

"Pastor, the months of July and August are normally slow with my business," he said, "but the day following my Faith Promise, I received an order for $24,000. And would you believe, the next day an order for $12,000 rolled in. That's unbelievable, especially in those slow summer months."

In **Texas**, a faithful, church-attending businessman, who had been baptized but had not received the Holy Ghost, committed $450 per month to foreign missions. The following week he purchased a line of product that he normally would not have been interested in.

Within only a few days, he signed a contract for the sale of this product that normally would have yielded a small profit. However, this time he made a profit of $250,000! His testimony?

"I *know* that this was a result of my Faith Promise!"

We can't wait to see what our next year's testimony will be!

Another **Texas** family owns a small business. In their first Faith Promise venture, the husband committed $250 a month.

"We were so blessed the first year that we committed to $350 a month the second year," the man reported. "At the close of the second year, the business grossed $500,000 more than it had ever before grossed. We had taken six vacations during the year. In previous years, we had not been able to take off more than one or two weekends per year.

"This year we increased our monthly commitment again! We can't wait to see what our next year's testimony will be!"

A **Florida** couple, challenged to give $25,000 to the church's building fund, struggled for a year and a half to keep their commitment.

At the end of that time, they started to build a home of their own. The bank approved a loan on the new place they estimated would cost $250,000.

After several months the husband remarked to his

wife, "We've not used any of the loan money on the construction of the house."

Then the Lord reminded the husband of something. "Do you remember what you did months ago for My kingdom? I just blessed you with ten times the $25,000 that you gave Me."

Two thousand miles to the north, in **Ohio**, a man had this Ephesians 3:20 testimony.

After that first Faith Promise year, I was amazed at the way the Lord blessed my family and me. You could explain it away by saying that we should expect things to be easier as our kids get older, and so forth. But we believe God has prospered and multiplied our efforts miraculously. In fact, we've never had such great results with so little effort.

We've had increased joy and harmony at home and among each other. We've been in a financial position to help others with significant amounts of money, which blessed both them and us. Every project we put our hand to surpassed our expectations.

I was honored as one of the top performers in my company. As a result of that, my wife and I went to Europe for two weeks, first class, all expenses paid.

My income has increased more than $100,000 over the previous year, beyond what we could ask or think.

First Peter 5:7 reads: "Casting all your care upon him; for he careth for you." Or, as Sister S. G. Norris paraphrased it for her students many years ago at the Apostolic Bible Institute in St. Paul, Minnesota: "Tell the Lord your worries, and let Him do your worrying for you." A couple in **Louisiana** did just that and received clear advice from the Lord. Here is their story:

A year ago my wife and I were fairly distressed over a situation we couldn't cope with. Every time I would get a raise, our rent would go up and destroy the raise. It seemed there was no escape from it.

We prayed and sought the Lord's will continually to help us find a small house to purchase so that we would at least be free from facing more rent increases.

Time went by with no results and then, finally, the Lord spoke to us very plainly. He told me to do three things. One of those things was to increase our missions pledge. We didn't know at the time how we could possibly do it, but we trusted God and increased our missions pledge at a time when even a dollar would be precious to us.

To make a long story short, God increased my salary thirteen times [over] the increase in our missions pledge and worked several miracles to put us in a house much nicer than the one we prayed for.

We don't say all of this to imply that we are rich and rolling in money, but we have come to know God for His great ability to supply our every need.

A **Kentucky** man and his wife also shared their experiences in giving to missions and how Faith Promise has blessed their lives.

At the time of my first Faith Promise, I did not have a job but decided to make a Faith Promise of $20 a month. Within a month the Lord blessed me with a job.

The Lord has helped us to be wiser concerning our purchases and we have learned to always put Him first.

My wife and I have tried every year to give to Faith Promise, but only in the past few years have we realized the benefits. Our first experience is from not being faithful to the Lord with our Faith Promise. We pledged an amount, but then during the year, we made one foolish financial decision and the rest of the year was a struggle. The following year, however, we made a commitment and told the Lord we would be faithful to it.

Since that commitment, we have doubled or almost doubled our Faith Promise every year. The Lord has helped us to be wiser concerning our purchases, and we have learned to always put Him first. We no longer live in an apartment; the Lord has blessed us with a house. We needed another vehicle, and the Lord led me to a very reasonably priced truck. God has also blessed me with a much better job that provides me with better insurance.

If that isn't blessing on blessing, what is?

Sadly, a young couple in **Texas** hadn't heard the warning in the Kentuckians and Louisianans' testimonies. They were both twenty-three years old. Married and fresh out of college. Filled with the Holy Ghost and acknowledging a call on their lives. She took a job as a sales rep for a land development company. He became a teacher at a Christian school.

Faith Promise time came, and they made a modest commitment. Her sales increased . . . and so did her missions commitment. Year one she made $250,000, year two she earned $350,000, year three her income climbed to over $500,000.

Then she began to miss church for work.

He decided to be a police officer.

They decided to back off their giving.

Now backslidden, divorced, and both remarried to spouses they do not love, they both told their former pastor that they went off track when they began to remove their offering from the altar.

In November 1993, an **Ohio** pastor felt impressed to have Faith Promise presented to his church. A great response amazed the pastor.

In the first month, the offering surpassed the church's Faith Promise commitment; they received a record Harvestime (Radio) offering of $1,300; and the church's income was sufficient to pay the church note for the first time in the church's history.

The second month, the missionary offering exceeded the first one.

The second year of their Faith Promise involvement, their offering climbed to eighteenth in the nation!

Months of growth followed, and they needed to either buy or build a new church. They searched for property and found twenty-one acres that they liked. The asking price was $599,000. They kept praying and believing.

The price dropped to $240,000, and the church bought the property at a savings of $259,000. Intrigued, the pastor checked to see how much they had given to missions. It matched almost to the dollar what they saved on the new property.

Then came the overflow blessing: a licensed electrical architect offered to do the electrical engineering that would normally cost up to $80,000.

The architect's fee? A flat $16,000.

Far to the west, a **California** church fell behind on their missions giving by $15,000. The pastor had been in a serious automobile accident and lay in the hospital as medical bills mounted. He had to sign over his assets to his wife but felt that the church should try to catch up their missions giving, so he asked a neighboring pastor to come and present the need to the church.

With the minister's medical bills soaring toward the million-dollar mark, the wife nevertheless committed $1,000 in Faith Promise toward the church's goal of reducing their arrears in missions giving. She had promised more money than they could afford.

Shortly afterwards he was approached by one of the doctors.

"Sir, I am not going to send you a bill for my services," the doctor said.

Then that doctor persuaded not only most of the team of doctors who had labored for his life to forgive him his medical bills, but he convinced the hospital to do the same.

Truly this was a million-dollar miracle!

Recently Jack received this letter from **Brother Ronald Hendricks**, pastor of the Greater Lighthouse Pentecostal Church in Madisonville, Kentucky, attesting the empty-basket-filled-to-overflowing-scoop-and-shovel return to investing in the kingdom of God.

Dear Brother Leaman,

Greetings in the name of the Lord!

Over sixteen years ago you came and brought a concept called Faith Promise to our church here in Madisonville that dramatically changed our church and also created a source of continual blessings and rewards to our church both collectively and individually. Our Faith Promise commitments continue to grow each year as our folks have witnessed how God has blessed those who have become a part of this tremendous opportunity to bless and be blessed of God.

One of my pastor friends had shared with me his testimony of how God had blessed his church with the Faith Promise concept and suggested that I call you. Like most pastors, the first question and fear I had was what it would take from our church. Like all churches, our church has many needs that we encounter just to keep the doors open, all of which is supported by the tithe and offerings. Let me tell you that none of those fears ever became a reality. Instead, the opposite happened as God opened the windows of heaven and poured His blessings upon us.

Faith Promise giving dramatically changed our church and created a source of continual blessings

Faith Promise really works! Let me say it again and again: Faith Promise really works and will bless any church. Testimony after testimony from our folks tell of how God has blessed them. Over the years I have seen folks go from no job to where they now have jobs with over six-digit incomes because they made commitments to Faith Promise when they had no jobs and no tithes or offerings to give. Others give testimonies of receiving pay raises and how God miraculously supplied for other needs because of Faith Promise giving.

Only eternity will reveal the extent of the harvest of souls brought about by Faith Promise giving.

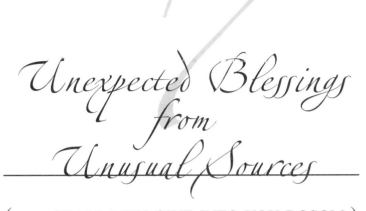

Unexpected Blessings from Unusual Sources

(. . . SHALL MEN GIVE INTO YOU BOSOM.)

God doesn't think the way we do. He says so.

He doesn't do things the way we do. He says so.

Neither does God think and do the way we think He should.

The prophet Isaiah quoted God: "For my thoughts are not your thoughts, neither are your ways my ways, saith the LORD. For as the heavens are higher than the earth, so are my ways higher than your ways, and my thoughts than your thoughts" (Isaiah 55:8, 9).

The key here is *higher*.

God's thoughts are of His kingdom, and for us even to approach the way God thinks, we have to think *kingdom* thoughts.

God encourages us, of course. That's why He admonishes us to "Seek ye first the *kingdom* of God, and his righteousness" (Matthew 6:33), and "Lay not up for yourselves treasures upon earth . . . but lay up for yourselves treasures in heaven" (Matthew 6:19, 20).

Think higher, in other words.

When we do that, when we rise above the world with its materialism, its prosperity, its greed for money and possessions, then the second part of that verse can be fulfilled: "and all these things shall be added unto you."

Added by whom?

"Give," Jesus said in the same sermon, "and . . . shall men give into your bosom" (Luke 6:38).

In other words, "men" would be God's earthly payback agents. And the giving would be "into your bosom."

The word *bosom* here refers to a custom among Oriental nations of making the bosom or front part of their garments large, so that articles could be carried in them, answering to the purpose of our pockets.

Sometimes, as in the following instances, the givers-become-receivers didn't know the "men" blessing them. In fact, the "men" didn't always fathom the depth of the blessings they'd bestowed!

"Found" money . . .

In **California**, a lady paid her Faith Promise for the month and then realized she didn't have enough money for gas the rest of the month.

Then a strange thing happened. She pulled up behind a car at a red light. The lady in the car ahead of her opened her own car door and placed an envelope on the walkway that divided the east and west traffic.

I wonder what is in the envelope? the lady from the church thought. She drove around the block and was surprised to find the envelope still lying in the walkway. So she drove around the block again, fully expecting the envelope to be gone. It still lay there, inviting her to pick it up.

Gathering her courage, she opened her own car door, reached down, and curled her fingers around the envelope.

When she opened it later, she found enough money to buy her gas the rest of the month.

Broke at the time, a **Mississippi** businessman accepted the challenge of making a Faith Promise of $20. The next day he drove a hundred miles to a job, and when he stepped out of his car he stepped on a $20 bill.

His buddies began to whoop and holler. "Boy, we can eat today!"

"Not with this money we can't!" the man replied. "I know where this money is going!"

He continued to give and give. Today he is a millionaire with a progressive plumbing business.

A **Tennessee** man didn't have his first month's Faith Promise of $50 and was praying about the need. The Thursday before Missions Sunday, he went fishing and found a wadded-up bill. Thinking it was only a dollar, he stuffed it into his pocket. When he unfolded it later, he didn't see George Washington, but Ulysses S. Grant. He'd found a $50 bill!

"Don't you think I can trust the Lord for my own Faith Promise?" a **North Dakota** woman asked her pastor husband.

He'd had Faith Promise presented to his church. He even had an amount in his mind that he wanted their family to give.

His wife, however, wanted to trust the Lord for her portion.

"But you don't have a job," her husband reminded her.

Nevertheless, she committed to Faith Promise and found the money hidden in many places after visitors would leave the house: under pillows, under the doily, once even under the toaster! She often chuckled at the unusual way the Lord provided.

No one seemed to know where the money came from.

Then again, some blessings lie in plain sight. A **Kentucky** man, laid off from his job and not knowing when he'd be called back to work, felt the Lord lead him to make a Faith Promise of $40 a month. The following day he drove to the church, entered the sanctuary, and walked to the front of the church. Later he left the same way that he had entered. There in the aisle lay a stash of currency and coin. He counted it and discovered that it amounted to exactly $40, the very amount of his commitment from the night before! He found out that others, including the pastor, had entered the church before him, and no one had seen the money lying in plain sight. No one seemed to know where the cash had come from.

The man was called back to work the same month.

A man in **Michigan** found a unique way to increase his missions giving. He put aside any money he found and at the end of the year gave it to missions. The first year he found $149. The next year, another man joined in giving money he found. That year they contributed $385 in "found" money. Now many people in the church are turning any money they find in to missions.

Taking a walk may be beneficial to a person's Faith Promise. An **Indiana** lady found $60 as she strolled through her neighborhood. And a groundskeeper at Oral Roberts University in **Oklahoma** discovered the amount of his Faith Promise on the bank of a stream where he was working.

Blessings from Outside Sources to Churches . . .

Churches, too, working as a unit, have reaped countless blessings. To illustrate, consider the Indiana congregation that had saved $2,500 toward drywall for an addition to their building.

When a missionary presented a special need, the pastor felt the church should take on the $4,100 cost of the project.

A short time later another church in that state called and said they would pick up the balance of the $2,000 for the drywall the church needed. God had seen a liberal pastor obey His direction and had responded.

A missions-minded church in **Missouri** needed to expand. For some unknown reason, the pastor's request for a construction loan was refused. The congregation, however, believed they should go ahead with the addition anyhow.

God provided in strange and unusual ways. Once, when the church needed money for electrical supplies, a stranger drove onto the parking lot and strode up to the preacher, who was working there with other men from the church.

"I want to contribute something to your building," the stranger said, handing the minister an envelope. The pastor thanked the man, who turned, climbed back into his car, and drove away.

The stranger's gift was a $700 check.

Every time a need arose, God met it.

A church in **Missouri** needed a new building. Although their Partners in Missions support equaled one-half the church payment, the pastor led the church to continue their support of missions. During the building program, outside sources contributed $22,000 to the project.

Outside sources also donated $8,000 toward the erection of a new sanctuary in **North Dakota**. The year before embarking on their building project, the small church had given $2,355 to foreign missions.

A church in **Texas** had been involved in Faith Promise for many years when growth dictated that they build a new sanctuary. The year before they started building, they gave $3,180 to foreign missions. The year they built, they garnered $11,000 from outside sources.

And in **Ohio**, a church did not have the $1,000 missions commitment the pastor had made. A Baptist lady came to church and gave an offering of $1,000, requesting the money be used for missions.

Blessings from Outside Sources to Individuals . . .

"What an amazing thing!" exclaimed an Alaskan pastor's wife when she opened a Christmas letter from casual acquaintances.

"What's amazing?" asked her husband, who had recently increased their giving to missions by $100 a month.

"This check for one thousand dollars," the woman said. "It's from those people who used to live near us. We hardly knew them, yet they sent us this gift!"

During the General Conference in **Tennessee**, the Lord touched the heart of a missionary's wife.

"I'll give to missions any extra money I receive," she decided.

In the next year and a half, she was able to give over $2,000 to missions.

"People would just walk up and hand me money," she said.

In **Michigan**, a new convert of two weeks made a Faith Promise of $20 a month. A couple of days later his boss told him that his raise had come through.

"But I didn't ask for a raise!" the somewhat bewildered man protested.

"Your friend requested a raise for both of you," the boss replied.

That day his friend called in and said he was quitting because he had gotten another job. The boss, however, did not rescind the convert's newly promised raise.

"I insist on paying the closing cost," the seller told the buyers, an **Iowa** couple that three weeks earlier had heeded the direction of the Lord when making their Faith Promise.

The closing cost? The exact amount of their commitment to foreign missions.

A pastor's son in **Oregon** had been tucking money away to buy a guitar. After a Faith Promise service, the young man willingly turned over his "guitar money" to foreign missions. Within months after the missions service, he was given two guitars.

One of the guitars was worth $2,400.

Although a single mom and struggling financially, a **New Mexico** woman put legs to her faith and made a Faith Promise of $100 a month for the next twelve months. The week after her Faith Promise, she got an unexpected order for materials in the amount of $1,230! God provided in one day her entire commitment for the year!

A Bible school student from **Wisconsin** made a Faith Promise of $20 a month. To support himself, he waited on tables in a restaurant. The month he made his commitment, a couple with two children entered the restaurant and sat at a table assigned to him.

They left a tip of $20. And they left the same generous tip on several return visits.

Halfway around the world, the Lord provided for four **Philippine** Bible school students in another unusual way. One of the students drove a tricycle to support himself, his wife, and two children; another had sponsors who reneged on their support; all four of them were deeply delinquent in their financial obligations to the Bible school.

Then they learned about Faith Promise and embraced it.

All four were invited to teach a *Search for Truth*

Bible study to a woman who, unknown to them when they began the study, was the executive secretary to a leading cardiologist in the Philippine Heart Center in Manila.

Through their association during the course of the study, she heard about the financial difficulties of the four young men. Then she told her employer some of the things she was learning from the Bible study.

This eminent doctor invited the young students to preach and to share the Word of God with him and some of his colleagues, granting each of them ten minutes to do so. Then the doctor called his secretary and asked for a check.

"As we all went home, we were thinking that maybe one month's tuition would be paid for," one of the young men testified.

After a few days, they were all surprised to discover that all their balances and accounts had been paid in full for the entire year!

"Through Faith Promise, God can touch unbelievers," they rejoiced.

During a weekend missionary conference in **Canada**, a man committed himself to supporting various projects that were presented.

"And Lord, I'll double my commitment if I rent that apartment of mine that has been vacant for three months," he promised.

He also needed to find someone who could truck out two loads of pulp that had been in the woods for a couple of months. If the pulp wasn't hauled out of the woods before it snowed, it would be spring before it could be sold.

The morning after the conference, a family called and rented the apartment! The tenant paid him three months' rent in advance, which was very unusual.

On Tuesday, a trucker called and said he could haul the pulp out that day. He took both loads before any snow fell.

On Wednesday the man sold a seldom-called-for part off a skidder. The chances of selling such a part were pretty slim. The buyer gave him $100 more than he was asking for the part. How rare is it for someone to pay more than the asking price on anything?

He could easily credit coincidence for one of these things to happen, but for three of them to occur in the week immediately following the conference surely showed God at work.

"Canned" and "Bottled" Blessings . . .

During a missions' conference in California, a lady gave $100 to a missions project. Between services she walked out, found a vending machine, and dropped in coins for a Dr Pepper. She drank the soda and looked for a trash container but couldn't find one. So, being a tidy person, she put the can in her purse.

When she reached home she noticed that the can had $100 stamped on it. Interested, she called the company the next day.

"The company is promoting Dr Pepper right now," she was told. "You are the lucky winner of one hundred dollars!"

Her blessing had come before she even left the church!

Although his job paid very little, a **Tennessean** was

challenged to commit $25 a month to foreign missions. A few days later he was eating lunch and drinking a Pepsi. He happened to notice that a message inside the cap stated he had won $100 for drinking a Pepsi.

"Hey, Bud!" he called to his friend. "I just won a hundred dollars for drinking a Pepsi! Would you believe it? It says so right here in the bottle cap."

"Lemme see that," Bud replied, reaching for the bottle cap. "Must be some kind of a trick."

"No, look here," the man insisted. "I'm supposed to call this number to claim my hundred dollars."

He examined the bottle cap more closely. "Hey, Bud," he exclaimed. "I won four tickets to a concert, too!"

When he got home, he called the number on the bottle cap. There was no question about the $100, but when he heard what the concert was, he realized that he wouldn't be interested in going to it. But he expressed his thanks for the $100.

A day or so passed. Then the soft drink company called him.

"You said you wouldn't be interested in going to the concert. Would you like the money instead?" he was asked. "The tickets are worth fifty dollars each."

The fellow did some quick figuring. Four tickets at fifty dollars each added up to $200. He received $100 from the cap. God had provided his Faith Promise for the year, all at once—in a Pepsi bottle cap!

Blessings from the IRS . . .

The IRS demanded proof of her charitable donations

from an **Indiana** woman. The IRS claimed she owed the government $796. She supplied more tax information than she had originally turned in, and the IRS refunded her $1,200. The same year an elderly neighbor died and left the saint $1,000 in her will.

"Brother Leaman, I felt I should make a Faith Promise of $20 a month even though I was in financial trouble," a man in **Ohio** revealed. "God met my needs, and the following year I received four thousand dollars back on my income tax. I wasn't expecting that to happen at all."

A senior pastor in **Ohio** committed $10,000 out of his retirement. Within the month he received a check from the IRS that he had overpaid his taxes by $8,700.

Social Security . . .

The Tennessee retiree fingered the notice he'd just received from the Social Security Administration. They informed him that they had made a mistake and his next Social Security check would be a certain amount. He had made his Faith Promise with a question in his mind as to how he could ever pay it. The answer lay in the notice he held in a trembling hand. The increase to his Social Security check was three times the amount he had committed to Faith Promise.

A senior pastor in **Ohio** asked the Lord to confirm the $50 a month he added to his missions giving. The pastor's wife received a letter from the Social Security Administration that they had overlooked something she was entitled to receive and enclosed a check for $630. Needless to say, the pastor received his confirmation!

The United States Department of Labor . . .

For five months a faithful supporter of foreign missions in Tennessee struggled financially after he was laid off.

Then he received a letter from the United States Department of Labor stating that in his inspector's position he was entitled to receive a check for $6,379.39. He and his wife were two delighted people. They had known nothing about the settlement.

Bank Errors . . .

"The bank made an error in the closing cost of your home," a Minnesota bank informed a pastor. "We will take full responsibility for the error."

The bank's error also reduced his house payment and insurance by $30 a month. His increased Faith Promise had been taken care of.

The Lord repaid a missionary kid in **Oregon** in two unusual ways. A few weeks after she'd made a Faith Promise of $600, her boss gave her a $500 check to show her his appreciation for her work. And twice since then, her checkbook was off $50 in her favor.

And Off-the-Wall, Who Would Have Ever Thought . . .

. . . that a family, because of the nature of their business, always had to borrow $30,000 to tide them over the Oklahoma winter months? They made a Faith Promise and realized at the end of the year that they hadn't needed to borrow money for the winter months.

A young lady from a Lutheran church in **California** visited a UPCI church in the East when a missionary

171

presented some needs for bunk beds and chairs for the Bible school in Guatemala. She returned home and told her pastor what she'd heard. The California church sent a check for $2,000 to assist the Bible school. A Lutheran church sponsoring a UPCI Bible school makes this a definite who-would-have-ever-thought story!

A **Texas** couple, after praying about their Faith Promise, agreed on the amount. Two weeks after paying their first commitment, she won three times their yearly Faith Promise in a contest.

Soon after the service in which a **Virginia** man had committed $25 a month in Faith Promise, a previous employer who was in trouble and needed him to testify in court contacted him.

"We'll cover your airfare, motel, and all expenses besides paying you two hundred dollars a day for the six days we need you," his previous employer told him.

From **Louisiana** a young man wrote:

At Missions Conference I was praying about how much God wanted me to give to the missionaries. I felt led to give $500. I briefly argued with God about it because I did not have $500 to be giving away. However, I have been blessed too much in the past and I know that God will always come through, so I went ahead and wrote my check out for $500.

Now I have to back up a little bit. About a year and a half ago I purchased a Web site domain name so that I could tinker around building Web sites. I paid $8 for that Web site name. The Sunday night after Missions Conference, I got an e-mail from someone wanting to buy the Web site name for $200.

I first thought that it was a scam, so I did a little research on Monday. I realized that the offer was real and I counter-offered it for $2,000. Well, Monday night I received a call from an advertising agency in Los Angeles, California. They said that $2,000 was more than their budget allowed. They offered me $1,000 for it. I'm not all stupid, so I took them up on their offer. I sold that $8 Web site, which was just a little hobby, for $1,000 on Monday night. That is some kind of profit!

I am overjoyed that God "out of the blue" miraculously doubled my [$500 commitment]. After that happened, I have had many financial blessings. Several side jobs have opened up to increase my earning potential. Because of the financial blessings I have received, I will be able to travel overseas to South Africa for the Youth on Missions trip this summer. This certainly did something for my faith, and I wanted to share it with you. We serve an *awesome* God!

The following drama from Michigan unfolds in three acts:

Act One: A couple on a narrow budget

carefully considered their Faith Promise renewal. The husband had had two back surgeries and was unable to work, so his wife was carrying the financial load. They debated their Faith Promise commitment because she was not earning even enough money to stay current on their bills.

"I thought it was unfair to expect such an awesome miracle from God each month," she said.

However, after fasting and praying about their circumstances, the woman felt she had direction from the Lord. She committed an increase and placed the whole situation in God's hands.

Act Two: The week before the first commitment was due they received a card in the mail from his shop. His former co-workers had taken up a collection for him.

"That had never been done for anyone as long as I had been employed at that shop," he remarked.

They were able to meet the first month's commitment.

Act Three: The big miracle came the following month. She worked in a highly stressful management position in health care. She was thinking of stepping down from her management position because an hourly position nearly equal in pay to her current wages opened up. The increase in hours would be counterbalanced by less stress.

She upset her boss when she let her know she was applying for a new position. The boss did not want to lose such a good worker and soon called her into the office.

"If you would be willing to stay in your present position, you'll receive an immediate raise," her boss told her.

The pay increase was a godsend. She could pay her Faith Promise while maintaining their household bills even with the husband still unable to return to work.

The following testimonial by **Brother E. D. Puckett** has been edited sparingly.

I began the Carrollton, Kentucky, United Pentecostal Church in October of 1978, and immediately God began to give us revival. After about three months we were able to obtain an old home-supply store to hold services in. This building we renovated in stages. The first stage gave us four classrooms and an auditorium that would seat about 125 comfortably. The second stage, about four years later, gave us an auditorium that seated about 250. We used the old auditorium for a fellowship hall and classrooms. At the end of the first renovation our indebtedness was about $100,000 and I was full time with the church. Our finances were a little strained.

At the end of the first renovation and having taken on several missionaries, I felt God begin to deal with me to have a Faith Promise service. I contacted Jack Leaman and scheduled him to come for this service. He came and, as we were walking into the door of the church that night, I told Brother Leaman to just preach and not do the Faith Promise service.

I had become afraid that Faith Promise giving would take away from the tithes and offerings that were then coming in. I scheduled Brother Leaman twice more and backed out at the last moment each time.

Finally, I scheduled Brother Leaman again and we went through with [a Faith Promise service]. From that time our offerings increased, our tithes increased, and the Faith Promise giving increased. God just simply began to bless our people. From then until the time I retired as pastor in 2003 we never experienced another financial strait.

We spent sixteen years in the storefront building and were debt free when the pastor of the Assembly of the Lord Jesus Christ church approached us about the possibility of merging the two churches and our assuming their debt. (He returned to his father's church in Louisiana.) They had built this beautiful building on 4.83 acres of prime land on the main highway, and we jumped at the chance to merge. We moved into this spacious building that seats 500-plus, paid off their debt, and sold our old building for more than their debt.

I sincerely believe that because of our missions giving and my giving the people of our congregation an opportunity to give through Faith Promise, God gave us this $1 million-plus property.

Don't be afraid to give your people a chance to step out by faith.

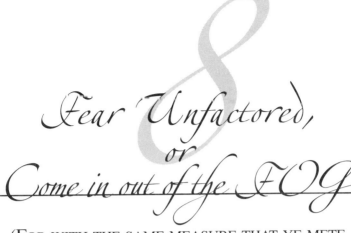

Fear Unfactored, or Come in out of the FOG

(FOR WITH THE SAME MEASURE THAT YE METE WITHAL IT SHALL BE MEASURED TO YOU AGAIN.)

Did you ever find yourself in a situation like one of the following?

You have sown much, but you have reaped little.

You eat, but you do not have enough.

You drink, but you do not have your fill.

You clothe yourselves, but no one is warm.

You seem to put your wages in a bag with holes in it.

Haggai the prophet thundered these words to the Jews who had returned from Babylon to rebuild the Temple—and let its foundations lie there, unexcavated for sixteen years. They had built themselves nice houses, but the real reason for their return to their homeland no longer seemed important, nor the work urgent.

Then Haggai prodded them to think about what they'd not done and to reestablish the house of God as the center of their purpose.

"Consider your ways," the Lord told Haggai to tell the

179

people. "Go up to the mountain, and bring wood, and build the house" (Haggai 1:7, 8).

In other words, think about what you're doing and get back on track. God's people had lost His blessing because they were living self-seeking lives.

"Consider your ways. Go up to the mountain . . ."

"I hate to admit that I didn't keep the Faith Promise I made last year," a North Carolina man admitted, "even though the Lord blessed me abundantly."

He had purchased two new cars and a number of other things. In thinking about it, he felt convicted, ashamed, and sorry for what he had not done. He renewed his commitment, determined he was going to be faithful to the Lord. He hardly climbed the foot of the mountain before going back to the core of the purpose for living.

God showered many blessings on the life of an **Ohio** man. Then the fellow decided that he could do a lot with the $200 a month he'd been giving to Faith Promise for several years.

Shortly after he began withholding from God, he lost his job. His pastor even asked other saints to bring food in for this family.

One day the pastor was praying about this family's need, and the Lord spoke to him.

"Ask the man about his Faith Promise."

"God, I never ask anyone about their Faith Promise," the pastor demurred.

Again came the impression: "Ask the man about his Faith Promise."

Finally the pastor asked the fellow about his commitment. The man confessed that the enemy encouraged him not to renew his missions giving, that he could do a lot for himself with that $200 a month.

"That's your problem," the pastor replied. Then he gave the man a quick Bible study on giving.

This man's trek to the mountain took longer, but he, too, considered his ways, recommitted to Faith Promise, and before long found a great job.

Paul warned the Galatians (6:7, 8) to "be not deceived; God is not mocked: for whatsoever a man soweth, that shall he also reap. For he that soweth to his flesh shall of the flesh reap corruption."

We tend to classify sowing to the flesh as all the horrendous sins Paul listed earlier in his letter to the Galatians: adultery, fornication, uncleanness, lasciviousness, idolatry, witchcraft, hatred, and so on. But the returned exiles in Haggai's day sowed to the flesh, too, in that they let themselves become enchanted and entangled with self, which, if spelled backwards—fles—is only a letter shy of flesh.

Unfortunately, the self, the flesh, intervened in a family that came humbly into a Pentecostal church. The family included two lovely teenage daughters who happily integrated themselves into the youth group. The whole family just wanted to do anything for the kingdom of God.

They had always given a small mission offering. Then along came a Faith Promise service. The Lord led them to commit $200 per month. They faithfully paid it. Their pastor noticed that their tithe increased dramatically.

The next year they increased their commitment to $500 per month. For three years their giving to various ministries in the church exceeded $50,000 per year.

Then they allowed themselves to become offended. They no longer laid a sacrifice on the altar. Gradually they ceased their Faith Promise and then their tithe.

The husband went to his business one morning to find that his partner had engineered for him to be forced out of the business. So the brother in retaliation swallowed a big loss and sold his part of the business to a third man with whom the original partner did not want to be in business. He invested the $200,000 he received from the sale into another established, profitable business. That business immediately went under because of embezzlement. He would later find out that not only did he lose his investment, but the employee who had embezzled the money had also opened up over $100,000 credit in his name that he had to pay.

Their oldest married daughter involved herself with another man. The youngest daughter backslid.

The parents left the church.

The man who was blessed with over $500,000 a year income now is driving a dump truck for the city. He withheld his sacrifice; God withheld His blessing.

A family came into the church in the midst of revival. Demonic spirits tormented their fourteen-year-old daughter. The psychiatric bills for the preceding twelve months had been over $50,000. But then they heard about the move of God at the Pentecostal church. Their daughter was delivered that night and they did not have to spend another penny on her therapy.

God began to bless.

They began to give. This family became the most generous family a pastor could ask for. When Faith Promise service came, they made a strong commitment. His business burgeoned. Over the next three years, they gave about $50,000 per year to the ministries of the local church.

But then they realized how much they were giving and began to back off. He called his pastor one day because he made a deal that lost him $150,000 in three days. The pastor encouraged him to recommit his giving. He did. Faith Promise came again and he made another commitment. He also promised $1,000 toward the startup cost for a church in a neighboring city, but when the offering time came he increased the amount to $4,000.

The next morning he called his pastor. He had received a call from a company looking for a particular inventory. It turns out this man's business was the only one in America with the desired inventory, and it had been sitting there for several years. The sought-after product had depreciated over several years until it was at a $0 value. The brother made a deal with the company for no cash but for $150,000 of stock that could be sold after six months. He was ecstatic that after his $4,000 offering he had been given this type of business deal. God had taken what was worth nothing and multiplied it to $150,000. This blessing replaced the $150,000 he had lost just a few days before.

Six months later he called his pastor.

"Pastor, I have a problem. Do you remember the $150,000 stock deal I made? It is now worth $385,000! The problem is I cannot cash it because the government will get too much of it!"

Several weeks later, he invited his pastor and another brother to go fishing with him.

"Can I sign the stock over to the church?" he asked both men. "The church could cash it tax free. Then the church could give some of the money back to me."

Of course, the answer was no.

The Lord spoke to the pastor. "Tell the brother that this $385,000 is a direct blessing from Me. Every penny is to be given back to Me. Then I will show him that if an offering of $4,000 could be multiplied into $385,000, I will multiply the $385,000 the same way."

The brother couldn't do it. It was too much money to give to God.

Two weeks later he called his pastor again and asked him to come to his office. He had sold the stock and decided to buy Enron stock and hold it for a few weeks. His profit in Enron would be enough to pay the taxes on both the Enron deal and the original deal.

The pastor sat in the man's office and watched the man's Enron stock devalue from $385,000 to zero in just a few hours.

Then the man found himself in the middle of divorce with a $600,000 divorce settlement.

The daughter who had been delivered from demonic oppression was being tormented again.

He chose to eliminate his blessing from the altar, and

it cost him $1 million, his family, and his daughter's peace.

". . . and build the house; and I will take pleasure in it . . ." was God's promise to the returned exiles. The Lord is evidently taking pleasure in the following "houses," for He has overtly blessed them.

A young man in **Minnesota** helped greatly in building God's house. He had given in Faith Promise offerings but never had any financial miracle happen to him like he heard about.

"But I've won five people to the Lord this past year," he stated.

Young man, that is what this is all about!

A **Michigan** church had a Faith Promise commitment of over $52,000 for the year. Four days after the commitment was made, a check for $50,000 arrived at the church.

In **Colorado**, a church was behind one year on their Partners in Missions. They "went to the mountain" when Faith Promise was presented and brought back stacks of "wood." God responded accordingly: The first month, eight people received their year's Faith Promise, while thirty-five received raises equal to their monthly commitment.

The pastor of a church in **North Dakota** related that his church fell behind one year with their Partners in Missions commitment of $380 a month and lagged three months behind on the church note. God impressed him to try Faith Promise. He did, and one year later they were caught up on their Partners in Missions, the church note, and had a little money in the bank.

During a ten-year period, a **Texas** church gave $250,000 to foreign missions. Then they remodeled the church, spending $250,000 in cash. The pastor gave credit to missions for what was accomplished.

A pastor reported to Jack that while his **North Carolina** church's average attendance of fifty-eight remained the same, their Faith Promise was up 20 percent over the previous year, the general finance had increased by 13 percent, and the tithes climbed by 24 percent.

"Pastor, what shall I do?" queried the church secretary. "We have a thousand dollars worth of bills, but only three hundred dollars in the bank."

"Send the money to missions," replied the **Ohio** missions-minded pastor.

A short time later, a saint in the church sold property she had been trying to sell for quite some time and gave the church enough to take care of the bills.

This **Florida** congregation tried to market their building for at least three years. They thought they had it sold several times, but the bank rejected the applicants. In January of 2005, they held a Faith Promise service. The pastor told the church that looking beyond themselves to reach out to a lost world would help them in selling their church.

Within the month following the service they sold the church for cash to a day-care center for $400,000.

"You can keep all the furniture," the day-care people told the church. "We can't use it."

The furniture, worth approximately $50,000, could

be used in their new church.

Leaman noticed plans on the back wall for a new auditorium when he preached a Faith Promise service in **Oklahoma**.

"Yes, I know we need a new building," the pastor admitted to the congregation, "but we are doing the right thing by having this missions conference."

Five weeks later a tornado chewed up the church building. The only part of the structure left standing was the three walls of the pastor's study, his Bible still open on his desk.

The insurance paid off, and the group erected and dedicated a new building one year later. The pastor stood before his saints on that Sunday morning and told the congregation that the new building was worth ten times what they had given to foreign missions.

A missionary from Argentina was the featured speaker at a missions conference in **Tennessee** at the same time that the church was saving for a new building. During the service the pastor felt led to empty the building fund and give the missionary the $10,000 the church had saved.

"I argued with God," the pastor confessed, "but I feel compelled to mention to you what the Lord has laid on my heart."

The church agreed to give it all to the work in Argentina. A few months later the highway department bought their church building, previously appraised for $70,000, for over $300,000. What's more, the building plans, valued between $25,000 and $30,000, were donated to the church.

"Reverend, we need a list of the church's assets," the loan officer said to the pastor of a **Texas** church when he went to the bank to apply for a loan to build a school.

"Well, we have various buildings our church has built around the world," the missions-minded pastor replied. "We've built churches in Brazil and Liberia, a Bible school in Kenya, and . . ."

"No, we need to see what assets you have here," the loan officer said.

"We don't have very much here," the pastor admitted.

So the bank refused to loan the church any money.

The church fasted and prayed.

The pastor took up cash offerings.

The money mounted up. And the school was dedicated debt free.

Have you ever heard of a church that was glad the bank turned them down for a loan? Well, now you have.

"Brother, you've outgrown this building. Why don't you back off from giving so much to foreign missions until you've built a new church for your own congregation?" A missions-minded pastor in **Texas** heard this refrain over and over.

"No, I can't do that," he always replied. "The Lord knows our needs. He will supply them."

And supply them He did.

In 1996, things started happening in this church, which had already given over $3.5 million to foreign missions.

A businessman in his church sold his business and gave the church $1 million. The church then bought thirty acres of beautiful property for $135,000, receiving a 10 percent discount because they paid cash for the land.

Then their old property sold for $2.5 million.

Indeed, the Lord supplied. Abundantly.

Still another church in **Texas** had been looking for property to build on but hadn't had much success. Though quite small, the group became involved in Faith Promise, and after their Missions Sunday, things started happening. They located four and a half acres that they liked, but the asking price was $250,000. They couldn't afford that; however, the pastor offered to buy two acres for $100,000. His offer was refused.

A few months later the bank called the pastor and offered the church two and one half acres for $50,000 on Interstate 35. They snatched up the offer.

They then started saving money to build. Six years later the state, in expanding an interstate highway, was buying property in the area and offered them $440,000.

They found five acres for $130,000 on a heavily traveled highway and are building the first stage of their church debt free.

When a minister was elected as pastor of a church in **Texas**, he found the church was supporting its Partners in Missions commitments out of the general fund. Unfortunately and quite often, the money left after church expenses did not meet the $250 per month obligation to missions.

The pastor initiated Faith Promise and urged the church to give more. The church hesitated to get further involved because of its own many needs.

The pastor continued to encourage them. "Faith Promise will take nothing from us but will add to us," he insisted.

The first year of Faith Promise they gave $10,000. Every year following they increased their giving. This involvement revolutionized their church. The monetary blessings have been unbelievable; they have not hurt themselves by giving. Their participation in Faith Promise has proven to be a blessing beyond reasonable proportion.

". . . and I will be glorified, saith the LORD."

This church in **Texas** has many testimonies of not-so-small miracles. The income has spiraled, revival has erupted, and they believe that if they do not give they will have a dead, dull, boring church. They continue to give so other souls can be won globally. As a result they have a church with an awesome youth program, a Christian school, a dynamic choir, an enthusiastic Sunday school department, and a packed-out church that is continually in revival—to God be the glory!

Then came World Missions Day, 2006. The church committed $48,000 for Faith Promise for the next year. The following blessings developed within seven days afterwards:

Day #1: A retired minister in the church made his small commitment and went to preach a funeral the following day. The folks there gathered around and stuffed $730 in his pockets. This is more than his monthly retirement.

Day #2: A young family that had been dodging the repossession man for their vehicle made a $40 per month commitment in a missions service. Two days later he arrived at his job in the garden department at

Wal-Mart to find that he was transferred to a nicer store and given a hefty $1,200 per month raise! Still in the garden department, he's one of the little guys moving potted plants around!

Day #3: A family doubled their commitment in the service. She was pregnant. On Wednesday she found out she was having twins. (Do you think they were glad not to have tripled their commitment? Of course, this is shared with you in humor.)

Day #4: A young family went to close on their new home. They had increased their commitment by $50 per month. At closing they learned that their escrow payment would be exactly $50 less than they had budgeted.

Day #5: A brother reports that on Friday he received his monthly commitment times three.

Day #6: A newly converted family had never seen anything like Faith Promise. They committed $150 per month. He runs a store for a national mattress chain. His commissions for the first week were more than he normally makes in a month.

Day #8: The Christian school added 10 percent to its enrollment. Wow! A 10 percent increase in students means a 10 percent increase in income, but there will be no increase in expenses to teach these children.

Now pastor emeritus of The Link Church in Canton, Ohio, **The Reverend F. Joe Ellis** established what he calls the miracle church. When you read the testimony that follows, you'll see why.

The First United Pentecostal Church, now called The Link Church of Canton, Ohio, was founded on July 13, 1980, by myself; my wife, Rose Marie; and our three small children, Angela, Joe, and Tom. The five of us were the founding members, but in just a few months a small congregation began to form. Because of its growth, the church was featured in the 1983 Christmas for Christ filmstrip presentation.

By October of 1993, God gave the Canton church an incredible miracle that many people to this day can hardly believe. Their first church building became too small. The church was in desperate need of a larger facility but had no money in savings to build or buy one. This was not because of bad stewardship but an act of obedience and faith. God had spoken to me in a vision shortly after coming to the city of Canton. He said that if we would continue to consistently give to world missions and not keep the money at home to meet our own needs, when our church needed a larger facility to worship in, He would give us a building debt free!

In the vision, I saw the inside of a uniquely designed sanctuary, with a horseshoe-shaped balcony that was packed with people from every nation dressed in their national attire. I saw myself holding a wireless microphone and preaching to the crowd standing in the middle of the balcony. The colors and the details seemed so real, right down to the dark cherry wood that lined the balcony, yet I knew I had never been in a building that looked like that. Excited about what I knew was a vision from God, I immediately shared it with my wife as well as the trustees of our church. We later shared it with the entire congregation. Little did we realize all that vision would come to represent.

Over time, several in the church began to doubt the vision, due to the overcrowded condition of our present facility. The trustees began to question the wisdom in our decision to give the majority of our money to world evangelism. They suggested that we possibly consider reducing the church's mission giving, to meet the church's present and future needs. The trustees were good, godly men with pure motives and intentions. They sincerely believed their pastor really thought he had heard from God. They just were not as sure since it seemed God had not provided them with a larger building.

Still wanting to believe a miracle was coming, the church unanimously decided to put the existing building up for sale, while at the same time checking out every facility that became available in the city. Two years passed with no buyers and no open doors. The entire church became tremendously discouraged and, for the first time, I began to doubt as well. Was what I had seen and heard in the vision real or just my imagination?

Yet, even in our discouragement, the church never reduced its willingness to sacrifice. In fact, just the opposite was the case. Giving to world missions was too ingrained into the culture of the church from its very foundation for that to happen.

Being challenged by the reports we had heard about a new concept of missions giving, we contacted Brother Jack Leaman from Foreign Missions to see if he would come and present Faith Promise to our church. On Sunday, September 13, 1992, Brother Leaman was greatly used of God in both services and challenged us all to give at a new level, trusting God to provide as we committed to give by faith.

Just a little over seven months later at the 1993 Ohio District spring conference in Toledo, Pastor Frank Poling spoke a word of prophecy to me that confirmed to us that the vision was real and it was shortly going to come to pass. The following Sunday evening after conference, I entered the pulpit with a fresh faith, admonishing the church to hold on to the promise. God had spoken, and it would come to pass. Without question, there was a fresh feeling of expectancy in the air. By Wednesday of the same week, a word of prophecy came forth and told the church to get ready to move because something was going to happen very soon. Just as God had said, two days later the miracle began.

Shortly after I returned home from the

church office on Friday, a pastor from the city called. He asked if we would be willing to consider a trade for a larger building. He explained that their church had declined in membership and their facility was much too large for them to maintain. They noticed our little building was for sale and were attracted to it. When he found out we had grown out of our facility, he asked if we would be interested in working out a trade.

Knowing what God had spoken just two days earlier, we agreed to meet him and tour his building. It was a much larger facility than ours (three times the square footage), less than a mile from our present location. He was right when he said they were unable to maintain the building. Nevertheless, the outside of the church appeared to be structurally sound. We had driven by the building many times over the years but had never been inside.

The moment I stepped into the sanctuary, I was overwhelmed with emotion. There it was, the horseshoe-shaped balcony and dark cherry wood. Those unique details were too prominent in the vision to ever forget. The only thing missing were the people who filled the place. My wife as well as the trustees who went with us were in awe of the place and yet at the same time were reluctant to get too excited. After all, we had looked at so many buildings before.

Unable to sleep that evening and after much

prayer, I felt God's assurance that this was the place that He had promised. It was the place that I had seen in a vision, and He had every intention to bring it to pass. The next morning, our trustees, along with my wife, assured me with confidence that this was the place that I had described to them in detail many years before. The following Sunday morning, the church unanimously decided that it was time to pursue the promise.

As always, the negotiation process had its challenges. But when they were over, the magnitude of the miracle was totally realized. Just as God promised, we traded our 5,500-square-foot building for a 17,200-square-foot building in an even exchange and were given our building debt free! What a miracle . . . what a God!

Many smaller miracles took place during the entire process that I feel are noteworthy to mention. For example:

The larger church building still had a bank note of $50,000 owed on it. Since we had paid our little building off several years before, the other church congregation agreed to take their debt with them and transferred their existing debt to the smaller building that only appraised for $42,000. That is unheard of!

Not only did we receive a title deed free and clear at the closing to a 17,200-square-foot building, we were also given a check of $1,250 to go along with it that had been donated for a new roof by the other congregation's members. Again . . . unheard of.

In obedience to God, we continually encouraged our young congregation to give consistently to world missions. Because of our decision to completely renovate the new building, we went to a bank to see about getting a loan for the renovations. Knowing we would need financial records, we researched our past giving records. We were amazed at what we found. From the time of our beginning to that date, we had given in excess of $72,000 to world missions while having a balance of only $800 in our own church building fund. The bank not only approved our request for a loan for renovations with only $800 in the church savings account but also appraised our new building for $720,000 . . . exactly 10 times what the church had given to world missions to date! In October of 1993, we took occupancy of the new facility and immediately began to renovate it.

Returning home one evening after a long day of working at the church, I received an anonymous phone call from a man who said he used to be a member of the former congregation of our now new building. He said he knew I did not know him but would like to share with me a vision he had during a prayer meeting in the sanctuary at their church just prior to the trade.

The man said he was so excited about what he had seen that he immediately shared the

197

vision with his pastor and the few people who were present. To his surprise, his pastor rebuked him harshly and said what he saw was not of God. The pastor said, "We are selling this building." The man, hurt and embarrassed, had not been back to church since.

Unable to speak because of the tears streaming down my cheeks, I listened intently to the anonymous voice on the other end of the telephone as he repeated the vision the Lord had given to me in vivid detail many years earlier. He then said, "Pastor Ellis, I know you don't know me. But I feel God wanted me to call you and tell you this vision. But He also said that I was to tell you that you and your congregation are going to be the fulfillment of that vision." What a confirmation! God always keeps His promise!

On Tuesday, May 2, 1995, our newly renovated building was dedicated unto the Lord. God had given us the miracle He had promised as a direct result of sacrificial giving to world missions. Our congregation was honored to serve as the host church for the Ohio District spring conference that week as well.

Pastor Harold Strange of Massillon, Ohio, was the dedication speaker. Pastor J. Hugh Rose of Jewett, Ohio, and presbyter of the section, performed the dedication. Many pastors and ministers who were present at the dedication also became part of the miracle by giving to our church a $17,000 dedication offering for the purchase of new pews. To date, that was the largest single offering ever received at any church dedication in Ohio. The greatest highlight of the evening, however, was to see those who were baptized in Jesus' name and filled with the Holy Ghost.

In February of 1997, God called The Link Church to a more direct involvement in international ministry. From nation to nation to nation is literally the calling that has since brought a clear understanding of the vision given to Pastor Ellis seventeen years earlier. Shaun M. Eller is now the pastor of the church, and F. Joe Ellis serves as the overseer, traveling extensively in North America and overseas as well. People from many nations of the world have been affected by the sacrificial giving of The Link Church of Canton, Ohio.

Today, flags hang from the dark cherry balcony, representing the twenty-four-plus nations the church has directly ministered in over the past eight years. This is not counting the many other nations and missionaries it has supported financially from its beginning through Faith Promise giving.

To God be the glory!

The exterior of the new church.

The interior of the new church.

About the Authors

John S. Leaman was born into a Pentecostal preacher's home to parents who dearly loved the Lord. After graduating from high school in central Ohio and from the Apostolic Bible Institute in St. Paul, Minnesota, Leaman was invited by R. G. Cook in Lancaster, Ohio, to be his assistant pastor.

Jack assisted Brother Cook for seven years, and then the Lord directed Leaman to start a home missions work in Wausau, Wisconsin. Five years afterward, R. G. Cook requested Jack to return to Lancaster. Later he assumed full pastorate of that church. During his final year of pastoring, the church was eleventh in the nation in foreign missions giving.

Then Leaman's life took on a new dimension when he was asked by the Foreign Mission Division of the United Pentecostal Church International to assume the position of Director of Promotion and Publication, giving direction to the deputizing missionaries across North America. There, he began promoting the Faith Promise program to churches that would financially support the missionaries and other projects overseas. Over the past thirty years, he has had the privilege of holding over 1,200 Faith Promise commitment services and seeing in excess of $54 million committed to reaching this lost world.

Leaman knows from experience that Faith Promise will bless any church that will step out in faith and let the Lord lead the congregation by being their financial advisor. He believes that Faith Promise will bless any church, pastor, individual, family, district, and country that will give God a chance to prove His Word.

 **Dolly McElhaney,** a graduate of the Apostolic Bible Institute, Macalester College, and Tennessee State University, began writing when Sister S. G. Norris recommended her to Edna Nation, a children's editor for Word Aflame Sunday school literature. Subsequently, over four hundred of McElhaney's stories were published. She has also penned two books: *Born With a Mission*, in conjunction with Carl Adams, and *Angel at My Shoulder: The Agnes Rich Story*, and worked as freelance copy editor for Thomas Nelson Publishers. For eight years she wrote articles for *The Print Out*, a bimonthly magazine produced by the Public Relations Department of the then Nashville State Technical Institute, and edited and proofread most of the material published by that school during the period of her employment there. She lives with her very understanding and supportive husband, Bill, and two horses in a retirement community in sight of the Great Smoky Mountains.